Promoting Yourself as a Photographer

Promoting Yourself as a Photographer

FREDERIC W. ROSEN

AMPHOTO
an imprint of Watson-Guptill Publications/New York

Edited by Marisa Bulzone
Designed by Jay Anning
Graphic Production by Ellen Greene

First published 1987 in New York by AMPHOTO,
an imprint of Watson-Guptill Publications,
a division of Billboard Publications, Inc.,
1515 Broadway, New York, New York 10036.

Manufactured in the United States of America

First Printing 1987

2 3 4 5 6 7 8 9 / 92 90 89 88

To Ruthie.

Remember—whenever we share a sinking rowboat,
make sure it's in shallow water.

Contents

CHAPTER ONE

What is Promotion?

The meeting took place in 1982, in New York City. It was indicative of how important promotion really is. The participants were Jean-Michel Cousteau, son of underwater explorer Jacques-Yves Cousteau, and executives of Nikon, Inc. The reason for the meeting was that the Cousteaus were planning an extensive trek to the Amazon basin of South America, an 18-month-long expedition to study the water, mineral and metal deposits, and animal life in that unspoiled area. The primary purpose of the expedition was to create a series of one-hour TV documentaries.

In addition to movie equipment, still cameras were required to record the exploration. That's why Jean-Michel, the brains behind the whole Cousteau operation, came to New York for that meeting with the Nikon people. But what Jean-Michel wanted was more important than mere equipment. He wanted Nikon to help *promote* the TV shows. He knew *promotion* was necessary for their subsequent success.

Nikon, in turn, wanted to help sell their equipment using publicity. Not surprisingly, an agreement was struck. Nikon agreed to supply the Cousteaus with cameras, lenses, flash units, and other accessories. This deal allowed Nikon to exploit their relationship with some of the most famous explorers of modern times.

What did the Cousteaus get out of this besides the equipment? Promotion. They got Nikon to promote the trip by issuing press releases that talked about the exploration, setting up appearances on TV shows, and sponsoring a much ballyhooed gallery exhibit at Nikon House of the photographs that would be shot during the expedition.

What's interesting about this deal is that even the famous Cousteaus realized the need to promote their work to the press using a camera company, and, by the osmosis of print and electronic journalism, to the public. They understood the value of promotion in selling their TV show in the same way that the professional photographer should understand the value of selling his work and his abilities through promotion.

Promotion can help a photographer do three things: Get more jobs, get more money, and gain prestige. Yet, for all its capabilities, promotion is an abstract concept, generally frowned upon by an unknowing public. In fact, promotion tends to have a negative connotation, something like, "Well, if he's so good at what he does, why does he need to promote himself?"

At the heart of these negative feelings is the criticism that society reserves for those individuals who are not content with their lot in life and have decided to take their fate into their own hands and improve on it. That's what promotion is all about.

Promotion involves selling a product to the public through the use of an organized and systematic program composed of a number of different elements, such as ads in professional directories and television appearances. The product may be anything from goods to services. An individual qualifies as a product, too. Regardless, once designed and implemented, the promotional program will achieve and solidify prosperity.

In a competitive marketplace, the photographer cannot survive without spending some time as a promoter. Making people aware of his skills by going after new jobs is the only way to get an edge. Promotion is not only the single most effective means for a beginning photographer to vanquish the competition, it is also the means for the more experienced photographer to catapult himself to the front ranks of his profession. Successful photographers understand the value of promotion and use it in their daily lives to reach the three goals—more jobs, more money, and greater prestige.

If promotion is so important, why do many photographers have trouble launching a successful promotion? Let's consider the reasons why promotion can fail to reach the stated goals.

During the 1973 baseball season, a relief pitcher for the New York Mets named Tug McGraw was asked by some reporters what his team's chances were of making the playoffs. His reply was the now-classic response, "Ya gotta believe."

The same thing applies to promotion and photography. Certainly, if you don't believe promotion will help your photography business, it won't. Second, if you believe intellectually, but not emotionally, the promotion will also fail. Why? Because, your heart isn't in it. You have to believe that promotion will significantly help you in order for it to work.

Belief, of course, isn't enough. Belief is nothing without knowledge and skill, both the knowledge and skill required to launch a successful promotion and then follow through and shoot the job.

If a promotion works well enough to get you an assignment, you have to possess the ability and talent to follow through on the laudatory self-assertions the promotion made, and shoot the job in a manner that satisfies the client. If you're not capable of doing that, you'll never get called back and the promotion will ultimately have to be viewed as a failure, a specific waste of time and money.

Perhaps the single reason most promotions fail is the lack of proper planning. If a promotion campaign is launched in a quick, haphazard manner, you will fail because things were not planned correctly. As an overview, a master plan for any type of promotion should include the following areas of analysis: what is your budget?; who is your audience?; when should you launch your campaign?; and, most importantly, what are you promoting?

START WITH OPERATING CAPITAL

Beyond lack of planning, the second reason most promotions fail is lack of money spent. By definition, paid promotions require money. Without money, there are no paid promotions—it's that simple.

Nothing in this world is free and to describe free promotions as being totally without cost would be to give a false impression. In comparison to paid promotions, the free ones require a lot less cash, but operating capital is still required.

For example, suppose you're trying to expand your business to another city and you've decided to use free promotion as the vehicle to promote that change. The principal elements of your promotional program are radio and TV appearances, as well as magazine articles, all about you and your work. Guess what? Your phone bill will be enormous. Ever try making long distance calls on a regular basis when you're doing it on your dime? It adds up. If you don't have the money to pay it, the phone company will flick a switch in their main office. Presto! No more phone service. How are you going to explain *that* to a client who's desperately trying to reach you?

Without either an adequate supply of operating capital or a positive cash flow, all of your promotions will fail. You've got to have some money backing you up. The time to launch a promotion campaign—free or paid—is when there's money in the bank and you're not worried where your next dollar is coming from. When your belly isn't empty, you can work with the confidence that comes from knowing your bills are paid and all's right with the world.

TIMING IS EVERYTHING

Timing is a big factor in planning. For instance, what good would it do for a sports team photographer to promote himself in the spring, when the teams have already been formed and contracts with photographers have been signed back in the fall? The time for promotion would have been the fall, when the teams were forming up for the coming year and the various leagues' board of directors were negotiating the photography contracts.

KNOW YOUR AUDIENCE

Nothing is more wasted than a promotion that doesn't reach the right audience. Knowing and understanding who you're trying to reach with your promotion is a key aspect of any marketing campaign. Perhaps it's an oversimplification to state that wedding photographers should be trying to reach people who are getting married, while commercial photographers are trying to reach advertising agencies, among others, but you've got to go beyond that—you've got to reach the person who has the authority to hire you.

In other words, promotions will also fail if the proper person, the one in authority, is not contacted. An example would be a promotional brochure sent to a junior art director at a large and powerful advertising agency. The junior art director will have to go to the senior art director for the necessary approval to hire you. However, the senior art director may be so busy that he can't make a decision on the spot and kicks it to the back burner. By the time he gets back to it, he realizes that he has already hired someone else for the job and tells his junior to contact you with that immortal line: "Don't call us, we'll call you."

Had you contacted the senior art director in the first place, and he liked your portfolio, you might have been a primary candidate for the job. If you had been chosen, it would have been the senior's idea, one that he certainly would give precedence to over that of the junior art director.

When you get a bit more specific about who to contact, what you're doing is getting your marketing down pat, because marketing is just as important as money, ability, and knowledge in making a promotion work. Your promotion has to be directed at a person who can hire you, which is the whole purpose behind the promotion in the first place.

WHAT DO I PROMOTE?

Good question. In the formative stages, before any promotion is launched, you're going to have to be introspective. Consider two questions:

1. What am I promoting?
2. What am I capable of promoting?

Tackling the first question, your choices will be:

1. Your abilities
2. Your photography
3. Yourself
4. A combination of the above

No, this is not a menu in a Chinese restaurant. It is merely a search to find what it is about you and/or your work that provides the best opportunity for promotion.

Abilities

Not all photographers have an equal amount of ability in producing photographs. What you have to do is figure out what you're best at photographically, and make that talent prominent in your promotion. Let's look at a number of different photographic abilities that you can promote.

Lighting. Art directors, in particular, point out that they like to use photographers who have a certain mastery in lighting their subject. This mastery, however, is not just evidenced in the technical sense. Rather, what they are looking for is someone who can do a masterful job technically, but just as importantly, give their lighting a certain distinctive style.

So, if you have a certain distinctive style of lighting, the selection of photographs that are used in your promotion should indicate this talent.

Special Effects. Today, photographers are using special effects more and more in their photography, from the wedding photographer who favors multiple exposures to the commercial photographer who strips surreal images into an otherwise ordinary shot.

But the photographer who is an expert at special effects manages to integrate the effect into the total image, so it doesn't stand out but rather becomes a part of the whole. This is a rare accomplishment. If you can do that—and you have the pictures to prove it—they should be a part of your promotion.

Graphics. Some photographers are experts at designing shots with strong graphics. That is, they can direct the viewer's eye through the frame by using line, shape, form, and color. If you have shots that are graphically arresting, include them in your promotion.

Color. I mentioned color a moment ago as an element of the graphic design of the frame, and it is. But color also belongs in a separate category.

Each human eye responds differently to color. For instance, if you were to put together the Muncel Color Chart, a standard measure of the eye's ability to discern color, you would see the way you perceive color is different than the way your friend perceives it. Similarly, some photographers use color better than others in designing a shot.

If you think that your mastery of color is above average, then make a special effort to use those grippingly colorful shots in your promotional materials.

Black and White. In the same way that some photographers are experts in color, others are experts in black and white. In fact, because color photography is much more common today than black-and-white work, a good black-and-white shot will grab the viewer's attention. I know many magazine editors who are always complaining about the dearth of good black-and-white work.

So, if your portfolio includes exquisite black-and-white images, they, too, should be included in your promotion.

Sense of Style. A sense of style is an intangible thing, based upon tangible things that set your work apart from that of other photographers. A sense of style is a mood, a feeling that the viewer gets from a shot; the ability to provoke an emotion, rather than a sleepy glance.

If there are shots in your portfolio that provoke an emotional response in the viewer, then you're showing a sense of style and those shots should be included in your promotion.

Problem Solving. Photographers who are expert at photographic solutions to a client's problems will want to promote that aspect of their work. Photographs that demonstrate this ability should be an integral part of your promotion. Over all the others, this problem-solving ability is something clients, in particular commercial ones, look for.

The Photography

The way to demonstrate your capabilities is through your photography. For instance, a promotional card that has your picture of a client's product in a graphically unique situation will show a prospective client how your creativity comes to the fore when helping clients sell their products. As you can see, ability goes hand-in-hand with photography. You demonstrate your abilities in your photographs.

But what if you are just starting out and want to launch a promotional campaign, but have no photography done on assignment to show how good you really are? The answer is a self-assignment.

Give yourself an assignment that will demonstrate your abilities. Take a look at the work of those photographers whom you admire. Get ideas about what you want to shoot, and then go out and do it.

With the photographs you produce, you'll now be ready to launch a promotion.

PROMOTING YOURSELF

Most of us are capable of finding a way to promote our abilities and our photography. But what about promoting ourselves? Don't we all have a unique way of looking at the world? Certainly, that unique look is what separates one photographer's vision from another. But there's something else.

Why you look at things in one way, and why I look at things entirely differently is what makes us, as individuals, separate and unique. We're not talking here of just having different photographic visions. We're talking about different *personalities*.

It is personality that gives resonance to our photography and, after an initial physical presence, it is personality that people respond to the most. What the photographer has to decide is how "out front" he wants to be with his promotion and how much of an active participant he wants to be in the promotion process.

Many people have all the talent in the world. Yet when it comes time to interact with others in business and social circumstances, they are in trouble. They have difficulty making eye contact, they have difficulty making conversation, they even have difficulty holding a glass without spilling the contents.

Now the latter may be an exaggeration; some photographers handle their business affairs well, go to social functions because it's part of their business, and have no problem juggling three glasses at one time. But that's, as I say, part of the business. To some photographers, promoting themselves is not.

The same photographer just described may not want to see himself promoted on a TV talk show. He may not want to see a picture of himself accompanying a brochure of his work, because he prefers that his abilities and photography remain in the foreground, while he is free to retreat.

The point is to be honest with yourself. Do you want to develop a public identity with your promotion? Do you want people to see you, to speak with you, to listen to you? Or do you want your work and abilities to speak for themselves? Once you make this decision, you will not only know what you want to promote, but what you're *capable* of promoting.

Should you decide not to promote yourself in a medium where you have to meet the public, you'll certainly be eliminating the opportunity to promote yourself through many of the elements of free promotion, especially TV appearances. Paid promotions do not require a public presence, until it comes time to show the prospective client your portfolio and you can get around that by having a representative handle that aspect of your work. Just realize that if you have self-imposed limitations, you're eliminating many promotional possibilities.

I personally believe that there is no greater promotional tool than personality. People want to know who is behind a photograph in the same way that they want to know who wrote an article or a book they've read. People are curious about people. The photographer can exploit that curiosity to his own advantage if he decides to not only promote his abilities and his photography, but his personality as well.

THE IMPORTANCE OF PROMOTION

Whatever or however you decide to promote, ask yourself the question: "How important is promotion?" The answer is your business has a good chance of failing without it. Of course, you may get lucky, but chances are good that you'll go under. There are just too many people out there doing what you're doing and to expect clients to miraculously discover you is a fantasy.

You have to go out and attract the business. It's like fishing: The bait is the promotion, the fish is the client.

Let's start reeling in the big ones.

CHAPTER TWO

Paid Versus Free Promotions

There are two types of campaigns that the photographer can consider: paid promotion and free promotion. In this chapter, I'll provide an overview of each type of effort.

The word "versus" used in the title above implies conflict, and there truly is a conflict between paid and free promotions. The primary consideration is which type of promotion do you attempt first, the paid ones or the free ones? The answer to this question is simple: the paid ones. The reasons are a little more complex.

Paid promotions are designed to show results in a quantifiable manner, as soon as possible. In other words, you keep track of how many people receive the promotional material. You query them by phone or on letterhead to find out if they're interested. If they are, you go in, show your portfolio, and—if you're lucky—you get hired. The whole process, from the promotion being sent out, through follow-up and the job offer can be anything from days to months. However, because a brochure, mailer, or other promotional material has a short life span (measured by the prospective client's attention span), chances are a successful promotion will see results within a few months. Not so with a free promotion.

First, free promotions are non-quantifiable. If you appear on a TV talk show promoting your photography, you can't just go out and ask every viewer of the show if they saw it and if they're going to hire you. In general, there's nothing to do but wait for the phone to ring. Remember, you may be reaching a larger audience with a free promotion, but it will not be as specific as the one reached with a paid promotion.

Given this set of limitations, it is the paid promotions, which see results in a shorter amount of time, that should be launched first. Ironically, the time when a paid promotion would be the most useful is when a photographer is just going into business or has been in business a short time and can use all the clients he can get. Unfortunately, it's in these lean times that there's barely enough money to pay for the electric bill, let alone a paid promotion.

However, a paid promotion is just as important as paying that electric bill. Whenever you need clients, it is the paid promotion that can get them for you. What good does it do lighting a studio that isn't in use?

The solution to this problem is planning. You absolutely have to budget money into your operating expenses for paid promotions, especially when you need the work. Whether you're just going into business, or whether you're already in business and want more clients, budget enough money in your operating capital for at least one of the paid promotions described.

You'll find that paid promotion is much more common than free promotion, because the opportunities for free promotion have really only existed since the dawn of the electronic age, specifically the common use of television, that began in the late 1940s. In contrast, photographers have been using various forms of paid promotion since the 1800s, when the art of photography was first invented.

WHAT IS PAID PROMOTION?

Paid promotion involves an expenditure of money to promote yourself to a smaller group of people than those that are reached with free promotions.

Where free promotions are designed to reach a large number of people, paid promotions are designed to reach a more select audience—namely the people who hire photographers to shoot jobs.

The elements of paid promotions are: logos, stationary, business cards, advertisements, flyers, brochures, mailers, calendars, posters, and catalogs. Let's discuss each of them.

Logos

Most photographers have a logo designed at the time they enter into business. If for some reason you haven't already done that, let's look at logos briefly.

Whether your promotion is a mailer, brochure, flyer, catalog, ad, poster or calendar, some place on it you should place your logo. It is your *original* logo that distinguishes you from other photographers.

If you're just designing your logo now, or searching for a new one, take a look in the color section of this book at the promotional pieces other photographers have put out. Study their logos. You won't want to imitate another photographer's work, but you can get some idea of what to do and what not to do, as well as what you like and don't like. Also, take a look at the logos that big organizations like NBC and AT&T use. Refine your sense of graphics. See what looks good, because what looks good sells the product, whether it be the services of a TV network, the phone company, or a photographer.

When you have some ideas, put them down on paper, then figure out how they can best be executed. If you have a graphic design background, you may want to do the mechanical—camera-ready art—yourself and then just hand it over to a printer for printing. If not, purchase the services of a graphic designer or art director. It should cost between $500 to $1,000 to have the logo designed and made into a mechanical.

Stationery

With a logo designed, the next step is putting it someplace, namely on your letterhead stationery and envelopes, which are used in correspondence with clients.

You've probably seen direct-mail promotions where one company or another invites you to send $10 in for a couple of hundred specially printed, personalized stationery and envelopes. You send the money in and a few weeks later, the package arrives. Opening it up, you find it's been specially printed all right, with smearable, low-quality ink, and the stock it's been printed on is one step above toilet paper.

The point is this: Stationery that contains your logo is just as representative of what you're capable of doing as any other form of promotion. If the logo looks elegant and it's been printed on high-quality paper, rag stock for instance, the client will think, "Hey, here's a guy who stands out from the rest."

Business Cards

Business cards are also a reflection of your professionalism. They usually contain your logo, name, profession—people use labels like "photographer" as a memory aid—address, and phone number. Again, if you're graphically inclined, you can do the mechanical yourself. Otherwise, call in the services of a graphic designer.

You'll probably find yourself distributing a lot of business cards at social gatherings, especially to prospective clients, magazine editors, gallery owners, just about anyone you meet in a social situation who can help further your career. I've found business cards extremely valuable not only in making a lasting impression, but in networking. People actually do keep business cards, whether in an organized file or a junk drawer. So, be sure to keep plenty in your wallet—you never know when one of them can help you get a job.

Advertisements

Advertisements fall into two categories: those placed by wedding and portrait studio photographers and those placed by commercial photographers.

Wedding and portrait photographers usually choose to pay for advertising in local publications, such as newspapers, or in their local *Yellow Pages* telephone directory. This type of advertising reaches the general public, which forms the core of their clientele.

It is only in the last ten years that it has become common for commercial photographers to advertise the work. This is due to the emergence of the *American Showcase* publications as the most commonly known directories of creative talent. Other directories, like the *Creative Black Book* and the *Madison Avenue Handbook* are also available for photographers to advertise in, but it was "Showcase," with its strong graphic presentation and eye-catching color pages, that convinced photographers to spend money regularly on space advertising, just like their wedding and portrait counterparts.

These creative directories are distributed free to art directors, art buyers, and others who hire photographers to shoot jobs. What the photographer hopes to do is have an ad that's strong enough to stand clear of the crowd and show him as a person whose work has some sort of quality, some sort of depth and talent, that his peers do not. Therefore, he will be the one whose page impresses the art director enough to get called in to show his portfolio and perhaps get hired for a job.

Many of the top commercial photographers in the United States have advertised in creative directories, including Pete Turner, Michel Tcherevkoff, Eric Meola, Don Banks, and Burt Glinn. Lesser known photographers also advertise. Regardless of a photographer's stature in the business, he has to appear to be successful by placing an ad so potential clients will think the photographer is as successful as the "major names" alongside which he appears. More importantly, art directors and art buyers *en masse* get the creative directories, and will have an opportunity to see and contemplate the photographer's work and possibly hire him.

It has also become common in the last few years for commercial photographers to advertise in the pages of magazines that art directors and art buyers read, including *Photo/Design*, *Chicago Flash*, *International Hot Shoe*, *Graphic Design*, and *Art Direction*.

Flyers

Flyers are printed pieces of paper or stationery, usually measuring 8½ × 11 inches. Their purpose is to advertise a wedding and portrait photographer in the geographic area that he services. Flyers can be distributed in two ways: one, by handing them out in busy areas such as supermarkets and shopping districts, or tacking them up on lamp posts and bulletin boards; and two, by sending them directly by mail to a list of former clients, referrals, and names culled from engagement announcements in the newspaper.

The big drawback with the type of flyers described is that they look cheap. Flyers usually have a lot of copy about what the photographer does, but rarely do they contain his photos, because the quality of the paper and printing process used is too poor for even adequate reproduction. If better quality paper and printing were used, the price of this type of promotion would go up considerably. Nevertheless, many photographers in this specialty like to advertise in this manner.

Brochures

This has become one of the more popular ways for photographers to promote themselves. Brochures contain a selection of the photographer's photographs and they are sent to prospective clients.

Brochures are meant to capture the prospective client's attention immediately, to make him aware that here is a new and special talent. It's the photographer's job to select the strongest images possible. The photographer will have only seconds to hold the prospective client's attention long enough to give the photographs a good viewing. If you can do that, you've got a chance to be considered for a job.

Mailers

The most common form of paid promotion, mailers are printed cards sent to clients and prospective clients. The cards contain one or more images that the photographer feels will be impressive enough to get work.

The cards can measure 5 × 7 inches, 8½ × 11 inches, just about any convenient size. Many photographers make use of reprints of their directory page advertisement as a mailer. Others develop campaigns with different cards going out each month.

If brochures are now becoming a common means of promotion, mailers already are. Art directors, art buyers, editors, almost anyone who can hire a photographer are inundated with them. That's why photographers are always looking for new ideas to stand apart from the competition in the client's mailbox.

It should be added that it's not a bad idea to include some sort of self-addressed, stamped postcard in the envelope with your mailer. By doing this, you'll be able to gauge and tabulate the prospective client's reaction to the piece.

Calendars

Calendars are among the cleverest ways to promote yourself. They are utilitarian and omnipresent. That is, they help the client keep track of days and dates and, because they are used for twelve months, the client or potential client will constantly be reminded of your work as each page of the calendar has at least one of your pictures on it.

Sometimes photographers will attempt to match the month to a seasonal image—for example, September might be accompanied by a shot of fall foliage and April by a photograph of flowers in bloom. These are general images. However, if you specialize in a certain type of photography, the calendar should reflect that.

Posters

Like calendars, posters are a promotional item with a long life span. They are meant to be a stunning visual effort, and are frequently used as wall decorations in art directors' and art buyers' offices. When that happens, the photographer's work is constantly on view, reminding the buyer that here is a photographer worth hiring.

Posters are among the most deluxe type of promotional piece. Certainly they are among the most expensive to produce, but there is also a great amount of prestige associated with their publication. However, your poster—just like any other effort you undertake—should be extra-special if you want it to stand out from the crowd and gain that place on the potential client's wall.

Catalogs

This form of promotion is not all that common and is actually done after-the-fact. That is, a photographer has been employed to create the photographs for a catalog that features some sort of product. The catalog that is produced not only promotes the product, but the photographer's work as well.

Often a photographer will agree to take the photographs for such a project for a reduced fee, with the additional compensation of a given quantity of the finished catalog. And while it might appear at first glance that shooting a catalog is more like a free promotion because the photographer isn't putting actual cash into the production of the piece, he is putting in his time to shoot the job and the fee may not be enough to cover the amount of time spent.

Some photographers also choose to compile a body of work into a catalog, which is then sent to prospective clients. What with the costs of color reproduction and high-quality paper, not to mention the services of a graphic designer to lay out the pages, this can become an expensive promotional piece. You might want to think twice about it before embarking on such a project on your own.

Which brings us to the second part of our discussion: free promotion. Much like the catalog example, free promotion involves little more than your time and a small dip into your standard operating capital. For that reason, it can be very attractive to photographers. Let's take a look at the elements of free promotion.

WHAT IS FREE PROMOTION?

I've said that nothing is free, but operating a free promotion campaign actually involves reaching the greatest number of people for the least amount of money—usually not much more than the value you put on your time and perseverance. The elements of free promotion are: articles, gallery exhibits, camera-company promotions, and TV and radio appearances.

Articles

Photography magazines regularly publish articles about photographers. These articles fall into a number of different categories, including the most popular ones: layouts and profiles. Photographers can also see themselves quoted and their work used in instructional articles. In addition, it's common for an article to have as its theme a subject that requires the opinion—and photographs—of a number of different photographers.

Photography magazines break down into two different types: consumer and trade. Consumer magazines are directed at the general public. They are available at newsstands and through subscription. Trade magazines are directed at the photographic community only. The photographic community includes photographers, art directors, photo suppliers, equipment manufacturers, educators, and students. Trade magazines are available free by subscription, which is obtained simply by writing to the magazine and requesting that you be added to their mailing list.

Whether you're published in a consumer or trade magazine, ostensibly there's no cost to the photographer. I say ostensibly, because there can be a sort of fee involved.

For instance, I know of a famous fashion photographer who was having a show of her controversial work at a New York photo gallery. As a guest, she had invited the editor of a prominent photography magazine in which she wanted coverage. She made sure to take the magazine editor to a grand and expensive dinner after the show.

If you were really cynical, you could say the editor was being bribed with good food and drink. I think the photographer was just being a good businesswoman by protecting her interests and making sure the editor's opinion was predisposed in her favor.

Gallery Exhibits

In privately owned and sponsored galleries, a photographer may see his work exhibited with very little personal cost. He may have to pay for the cost of invitations for the opening night party, as well as the cost of the party itself, but that's it. However, gallery co-ops require a photographer to pay a fee to join the gallery in return for a gallery exhibit at various times.

Photographers like to have their work exhibited in galleries. First, it's a way to sell their work to collectors and others interested in purchasing prints. Second, they can use the opening night party to promote themselves to current and potential clients. If the show is well-reviewed by critics who write for newspapers and magazines, additional positive interest in the photographer and his work will be generated.

Camera-Company Promotions

Camera companies make money by selling cameras and equipment. One of the ways they convince consumers to go out and buy their product is to get a professional photographer to promote the equipment. This is the most complex form of free promotion.

Essentially, the photographer is endorsing the product for a fee, and that endorsement is contained in advertisements for the product. Also, the photographer will endorse a product in press releases, which the camera company distributes to consumer and trade photography magazines, with the hope of having them published.

Other times, photographers may have their name used in a press release, where they do not come right out and endorse the product, but state they are using it for an unusual assignment. In such cases, the photographer has probably been given or loaned the equipment on a long-term basis, for this quasi-endorsement.

The principal benefit of the camera company promotions described is that the camera company takes the burden of promotion off the photographer's shoulders and does it for him—at no charge.

TV and Radio Appearances

Andy Warhol once said that sometime in the future, everyone will be famous for 15 minutes. Actually, TV time constraints make that an optimistic estimate.

Consider that segments of most TV interview shows run five to seven minutes. Guests, regardless of occupation, frequently occupy just one segment. There goes Andy's prediction. Yet in those fleeting minutes, the guest reaches millions of people. This is the power of TV: delivering a mass audience. That's why photographers should look very seriously at a TV appearance or appearances as a viable promotional form.

Like other forms of free promotion, it is hard to quantify the results of a TV appearance. Still, not all promotion has to be quantifiable, especially when you're reaching such a large audience.

The same logic holds true in terms of a radio appearance. Compared to TV, you're reaching a smaller audience. However, you're still communicating with thousands of people.

The advantage of radio over TV is that radio shows allow you more time to talk about your work. The drawback is that radio is an *aural* medium. Unlike TV, you won't be able to influence anyone with your photographs or your presence, only your voice.

If a successful TV appearance is judged on the basis of how your personality comes across into people's living rooms, then a successful radio appearance, given the length of time available (sometimes as much as 60 minutes) should be judged on your ability to communicate ideas in a coherent manner, especially those that are behind the success of your work.

KEEP A POSITIVE ATTITUDE

If the opportunities for free promotion abound—and they do—why don't more photographers take advantage of them? Of course the results are unquantifiable, but it goes deeper than that. Most photographers do not understand free promotion, let alone its benefits. Understand it and you can exploit it for your own gain.

Don't take the attitude that you're not good enough to endorse a company's product, or be a guest on a local TV show. If you feel that way about yourself and your work, no one will want you—especially not a client. Taking full advantage of the opportunities free promotion has to offer requires confidence in your abilities and this confidence is the key to a successful free promotion.

CHAPTER THREE

Spending Money to Make Money

The success of a paid promotion will be determined by a number of factors, not the least of which is luck. For example, an art director needs a photographer to shoot a certain job, but can't find one whose style matches the way he envisions the photographs. Then, your mailer happens to arrive on his desk. He likes what he sees, thinks you can shoot the job for him, calls you in, likes your portfolio, and you get the job. Okay, that's luck—and the odds of such a scenario occurring are slim. But what isn't luck is the mailer being impressive enough to inspire the art director to give you a call in the first place. That's the result of good promotion.

Since a high-quality, well-planned promotional campaign is so important, extra care should be taken each step of the way. A successful campaign doesn't have to cost your last dime, but if you have the money allotted in your budget, you shouldn't try to cut corners. Hiring the services of graphic designers and professional consultants is well worth the expenditure. These people are experts at creating promotions that will catch the eye of the prospective client and make him want to hire you.

However, depending on the status of your budget and your photographic career in general, you may not have the money to hire a promotion specialist. In that case, we'll go through the various paid promotional elements one by one and you can consider which of these you would be capable of tackling by yourself.

SPACE ADVERTISING

When we talk about advertising, the first reaction among photographers is to purchase a page in one of the professional directories. However, depending on the type of work you do, these large annual books may not be appropriate for your promotion plan. Consider starting out with something that might be a bit easier: Take an ad out in a magazine.

Specifically, place an ad that contains copy rather than images to promote your services. The ad can go in local publications, including newspapers, supermarket shopper-type newspapers, or regional publications.

Since the majority of these publications go to the general public, it will be wedding and portrait photographers who'll want to take the most advantage of this type of advertising. Commercial photographers who specifically want to service advertising agencies and their clients would, by and large, be wasting their money in this venue.

The advantage of choosing an advertising plan like this is that you don't have to worry about laying out an ad, because the copy is selling your service. Of course, you'd be better off hiring a professional writer to write the copy, but the services of writers cost a lot less than other creative people, like graphic designers. For instance, if you have an ad that is going to run 50 words, a professional writer should not charge you more than a few hundred dollars. Compare that to the higher fees quoted by designers later in this chapter and you've already cut your expenses before the ad is bought or even appears.

To purchase an ad, call the magazine or newspaper directly and ask to speak to a space salesman. When you have him on the line, ask him what the cost is for the following rates: one time, five times, and ten times. The more times you place the ad, the cheaper it gets.

For classified ads, which are the type we're talking about, each publication has its own limits on space. Usually, classified ads run about 45 to 50 words, with an additional charge for each word over a given quantity. The idea is to keep the cost down by writing an ad that is concise, making sure, of course, to have your name, address, and phone number displayed prominently.

One photographer who went the classified route with mixed

success was Rudy Pollak. Pollak owns Dino Custom Color Photography, a wedding and portrait studio in Elmhurst, New York. Pollak was getting tired of shooting just weddings and portraits and had decided to expand into a burgeoning area: boudoir photography.

For the uninitiated, boudoir photography is the process of taking portraits of women in provocative garments, using the lighting and posing techniques of fashion photography. The women then present the portrait as a present to their husbands or boyfriends. Folks, I'm only a reporter. I don't make this stuff up and frankly, a lot of photographers are doing quite well specializing in this type of photography.

"One of the reasons I decided on boudoir photography was because of a survey that Eastman Kodak had come out with," says Rudy Pollak. "The survey said that 70 percent of the portrait market was going to the department stores. If that was true, it would be hard to compete. I needed something that they couldn't do and since boudoir photography is popular, I thought I'd give it a try." But, in his haste to get into it, Pollak violated the cardinal rule: He didn't target his audience.

Pollak's first ad was in *New York* magazine, a decidedly upscale publication. It appeals to "Yuppies," many of whom have difficulty shedding their briefcases at the end of a day, let alone their inhibitions and their clothes. Nevertheless, Pollak took space out in *New York*, which cost $300 for a two-line ad that ran for six weeks.

The result was over 100 calls from people who saw the ad, but very little business. "*New York* was a bomb," says Pollak.

The ad was not successful for two simple reasons. First, the audience he was trying to reach, the average person who wants to engage in a fantasy of looking like Joan Collins, doesn't read *New York*. Second, the ad was too small to attract attention. As Pollak himself points out, "It's impossible to make money from an ad in that magazine unless it's large enough for people to read without difficulty."

But the seed had been planted and Pollak decided to pursue advertising further. The next time, he tried *Newsday*, a newspaper that serves the suburban community on Long Island, east of New York City.

"I don't think the upper-middle-class market in Manhattan that reads *New York* really goes for boudoir photography. However, *Newsday's* readers really responded well to the ad."

Certainly, Pollak had done a better job in the latter case of targeting his audience. In addition, *Newsday* charged a lot less money for a lot more copy, sometimes as little as $10 for a filler ad.

"Out of 100 calls from the first *Newsday* ad, I got 10 new clients," Pollak says proudly. "I also got referrals from the new clients. As for the people I wound up photographing, 80 percent had good bodies and the other ones were challenges."

Pollak now has decided to launch two new advertising campaigns, involving parents and pets.

"The tag lines on one of the ads will say, 'Do you have a portrait of your parents?' I came up with the idea after customers came into the studio asking for restoration of old pictures of parents who had died. I would tell them, 'Why didn't you bring them in to have their picture taken, instead of having to rely on faded photographs for memories?' "

The other new promotion Pollak is working on is pictures of pets. "I put four ads in *Newsday* advertising us as pet photographers. I got a referral from each of those ads. In fact, I'm shooting a pet portrait tonight."

Pollak, who used to be in advertising himself and writes all of his ads, is going to continue his *Newsday* ads as a way of promoting himself out of the wedding and portrait market. But in the meantime, he won't neglect the bread-and-butter of his trade either in his advertising plans—in a manner of speaking.

"There's a new magazine out called *New York Wedding*. It's one issue for the whole year. I'm paying $500 for a quarter-page ad. What I'm advertising is boudoir photography. A gift from the bride to the groom."

Yellow Pages. Of course, the most basic type of space advertising for any photographer, but particularly wedding and portrait photographers, is a listing in the telephone directory *Yellow Pages*. *Yellow Pages* advertising falls into two basic categories: a line listing and a full ad. Listings for this particular field will fall under the heading in the *Yellow Pages* that reads "Photographers—Portrait," which also includes wedding photographers.

The basic line listing includes the name of your studio, address, and phone number. It might read as follows:

ROBERT CUMMINGS PHOTOGRAPHY
852 Second Street 555-1212

For an additional cost (and costs are higher in urban areas) you can have your listing in bold-face type on two lines, which might look like this:

ROBERT CUMMINGS PHOTOGRAPHY
852 Second Street 552-1212

For a little more money, you may also include a description of your services, using three or more lines, which would be similar to this:

ROBERT CUMMINGS PHOTOGRAPHY
Specialists in Wedding Photography
852 Second Street 552-1212

And if you have even more money in your promotional budget, you can buy an ad that takes up more column space. Typically, wedding and portrait photographers who want a larger ad go for one that measures 1 × 2 inches. The copy might read, in a rectangular format, as follows:

ROBERT CUMMINGS PHOTOGRAPHY
WEDDING SPECIALIST
The greatest love story ever told . . .
The Ultimate in Bridal Photography
852 Second Street 555-1212

This type of ad is guaranteed to stand out from the rest.

DIRECTORIES

I've discussed advertising outside of professional directories simply as an alternative, especially for those photographers who don't immediately have the money to pay for an ad that includes color photographs. However, commercial photographers, by far, will want their paid advertising to appear in the professional directories, which are read by art directors and others who hire photographers for jobs.

The rates for the directories are discussed later in this chapter. For now, I'd like to talk about how to go about placing an ad in these directories. Essentially what you're doing is buying a page or more of space that contains your photographs arranged in an eye-catching manner.

I think it's a good idea to have an art director or graphic designer design your directory page for you. However, if times are tight monetarily, you may not be able to afford the services of this type of professional. In addition, many of these publications have people on staff who offer advice and guidance. Here's some specific tips about placing an ad from four of the more prominent professional directories.

The Creative Black Book

Founded in 1969, the *Creative Black Book* is a directory of talent for services that art directors might have use for, including illustrators and photographers. Within this context are ads by photographers. Like photographers who advertise in other publications, they are trying to call special attention to their work.

Linda Kaufman, the sales manager of the *Creative Black Book*, has some general advice for photographers who are looking for a place to advertise.

"Before advertising, a photographer should ask himself these questions:

1. Where is it (the directory or sourcebook) going?
2. How is it being used?
3. How is it perceived?
4. How easy is it to use?

5. Are the people who publish the book in tune with the needs of the photography industry?

6. Are the other ads by photographers in the top rank of their profession?

7. How good is the design and promotional advice that the publication gives you?

"We recommend tracking the effectiveness of an ad," Kaufman continues. "One way to do this is—when someone calls up cold—find out how they know about the photographer. The rep, studio manager, whoever answers the phone, should make a note when a cold call is the result of an ad. This way, you know how effective it is."

Kaufman also has another useful suggestion, based upon experience. "Some photographers who advertise in the *Creative Black Book* use a special phone number in the ad. The phone line in the studio that corresponds to this number only receives calls as a result of the number in the ad, thus providing an exceptional tracking device."

American Showcase

By far, *American Showcase* is the most well-known professional directory available. Actually, there are three American Showcase directories: *American Photography Showcase*, *American Illustration Showcase*, and *American Corporate Showcase*.

Commercial photographers tend to advertise in the first publication, illustrators in the second, and corporate and annual report photographers in the third. The company's advice is the same, regardless of the publication you choose to advertise in.

"Many photographers come to us from scratch and ask us to help them. Of course, we do," says Kyla Kanz, a production manager for the company.

"If you live in New York City, it's easy. You just make an appointment, come in, and talk to the people in our design department. If you're out of town, you contact one of our regional sales reps, who'll help you.

"Essentially, what we try to do is help the photographer specify the aim of his ad. We'll help target the market he wants to reach. Then we can tell him what types of photographic styles and content are current, which is what clients are looking for and also, what types of photos stand out."

Another thing the "Showcase" staff looks for is whether something unique about the photographer's style can be played up in the ad. "Showcase" will also offer advice to the photographer who wants to use his ad to change his photographic specialty.

"If the photographer doesn't have a strong portfolio to back up the claims he makes in his ad, we'd recommend that he wait until his portfolio is built up enough in the area he's trying to get into, before advertising himself as an expert. Or, we might recommend that he take out a page that shows a number of different styles of photography, so he's not claiming to be an expert in any one category where the work does not exist to back up the claim," Kanz points out.

At the same time, she cautions against using a hodgepodge of images that might be too confusing to the prospective client. There's a fine line between proving to an art director that you can shoot a variety of jobs in different categories of photography and confusing him with too many images. The deciding factor will be the strength of the photographs. This is a point that Kanz expands upon.

"Play up the photography in your page and not the *design* of the ad. It's the images that sell you, not the design.

"We'll also tell you which 'take' of a specific image is best, which images overall are best for the page, which colors work best on the page, and whether to include your logo or not."

Kanz says that the two most common mistakes by photographers who advertise in *American Photography Showcase* are: one, showing too many photographic styles in the images selected and two, showing only one photograph.

The first mistake has already been addressed. As for the second, Kanz says that by using only one image, no matter how strong, the potential client will probably say something like, "He got lucky with one. So what else does he do?" By that time, he's already turned the page and is looking at another photographer's work.

One of the drawbacks of advertising in *American Photography Showcase* is that there are no demographics to show the effect of the ads.

"We don't get feedback when things go well, only when they go bad," muses Kanz. "Sometimes, however, repeat clients will say, 'This ad worked really great.' "

Despite this drawback (which shouldn't be overlooked because you really want to know an ad's effect), the advantages outweigh the disadvantages. One of the advantages is that *American Photography Showcase* and its sister publications are printed in Japan and the Japanese are known for the quality of their color separations. Also, everyone who advertises gets color proofs to approve before anything is actually printed. And *American Showcase* staff is present in Japan during the actual printing process, constantly checking to make sure color reproduction is accurate.

There are two other points about *American Showcase* that will be of interest. You can ask for a distribution list, which will tell you to whom the publication is sent. The list can be purchased separately, even if you don't buy an ad.

Second, all the *American Showcase* publications have gray pages, located in the back of each directory. These gray pages list the phone numbers of photographers and illustrators broken down by region. While advertisers' listings are highlighted in bold face, those who don't buy pages may also be included—*for free*.

All you do is call *American Showcase* in New York City or your regional sales rep. Tell them you want to be listed in the gray pages, give them the information and the next time the directory comes out, your name will be included. This also gets you on the salesperson's contact list, which means that *American Showcase* will keep in close touch.

Advertising Photography In Chicago

Advertising Photography In Chicago is a regional directory that services the Midwest, especially Chicago. The publication also has some limited national circulation.

What makes this book unique among the other promotional directories is its physical set-up. Explains Dawn Henninger, one of the company's account representatives:

"The whole concept of *Advertising Photography In Chicago* is to sell ad pages with adjoining copy. That is, each advertiser also gets an adjacent page with editorial copy. So, the ad is on the right-hand page, for maximum visibility, and the copy is on the adjoining left-hand page."

Because the format is standardized, what is contained on the editorial page are photographs that are personal favorites of the photographer, which he comments on in the text. There's also a photograph of the photographer, all of which helps to build what is, in essence, a yearbook of midwestern photographers, each having a separate identity. The content of the right-hand page, the actual ad with eye-catching photographs, is another story.

"The first thing I should mention," Henninger states, "is that our client base is more developed in the Midwest. We only solicit Chicago photographers because we are showcasing Chicago talent to the nation.

"As to the photographers advertising, the bulk of our advertisers are commercial photographers. Secondary customers are photographers shooting for stock. We also publish ads from stock houses and photo labs. All of them are trying to reach our audience: creative professionals like art and creative directors and designers."

In addition to publishing color ads, *Advertising Photography In Chicago* also publishes black-and-white ads, which is especially helpful to those photographers who build their print promotions around black-and-white photography. Of course, the black-and-white ads cost less than the color ones (see listings later in this chapter).

"When we first approach a photographer about advertising, or they approach us," says Henninger, "we go over a prepared list of questions that are designed to help the photographer create an ad that's eye-catching. We then look through their portfolio and help the photographer select images that best represent their talents and the image they're trying to project.

"What I find is that photographers are used to dealing with film and what the image looks like on film. Advertising is a different process, which involves ink on paper. There's a constant conflict between the perception of how a photographer expects the film to look on the printed page and the way it actually looks. We try to point out that film has more clarity than a printed piece.

"When we work with a photographer who's done little or no advertising," Henninger continues, "we help him choose images that will reproduce well, rather than have them just be his favorites.

The more subtle an image is in graphic design, including color, the more difficult it is to print it clearly."

Once the images are chosen, the photographer is given art boards. He is asked to provide the layout and the final choice of transparencies. Therefore, the photographer has to provide camera-ready art. This can be a problem if he knows nothing about graphic design or doesn't have access to a graphic designer. The way of solving this problem is by looking at successful ads, to which Henninger and the other account representatives will give the photographer access. The photographer can then, essentially, copy the layout of a successful ad. And how does *Advertising Photography In Chicago* know when an ad is successful? Henninger responds:

"We get feedback. Photographers drop us a note to tell us what progress they're making. Or I may be calling on one of my accounts, which I do all the time, and I'll get some response. This way, we can keep track of the ads."

Like *American Showcase*, *Advertising Photography In Chicago* is printed in Japan. The photographer gets one press proof of his ad on which to note corrections. *Advertising Photography In Chicago*'s publisher and production manager then travel to Japan to oversee the actual printing process and maintain quality control.

The principal drawback of this publication is that it doesn't provide a mailing list, so the advertiser can never be sure of who exactly his ad is reaching. The publication does provide a circulation card, with some general information about its readership.

When asked to comment on the two most common mistakes photographers make when designing ads, Dawn Henninger replied: "One, photographers become too involved with the design of the ad, which sometimes overshadows the photography and two, photographers often have unrealistic expectations of what advertising can do for them." She elaborates:

"I realize it's an investment in their business, but photographers can spend an incredible amount of money on one ad rather than planning a promotional strategy over the longer term for an overall campaign.

"I have a Bachelor of Science in advertising from the University of Illinois at Champaign/Urbana. The first thing you're taught in the advertising sequence is that advertising consistently is more effective than doing a fancy one-shot. That's why my best advice to photographers when they advertise is not to spend their entire promotional budget on one vehicle."

Henninger wouldn't say it, but there is an emotional context to an ad by a photographer that contains just one photo. It appears to be either an act of desperation: "See, see, I told you I could do it!" or an arrogant, aggressive statement of the photographer's qualifications: "I don't have to advertise with more than one image. I'm so good, the one image says it all."

Take Henninger's advice. Use more than one image, and don't spend your whole budget on one ad. No matter how good it is, it may not get you enough business to have justified the cost.

Madison Avenue Handbook

The *Madison Avenue Handbook* is the oldest directory in point of service. Established over 30 years ago as a model's directory, it developed down through the years as a sourcebook of professional photographers, with ads aimed primarily at art directors and creative directors.

For a time, it was quite successful fulfilling the latter function. But with the emergence of the *Creative Black Book*, *American Showcase*, and other directories, the competition forced the *Madison Avenue Handbook* to realign their marketing strategy. They broadened their ads, which include color and black-and-white pages, as well as bold-face and regular listings, to include creative professionals working in a variety of areas.

A current copy of the *Madison Avenue Handbook* will include ads from: photographers, illustrators, film and video production people, audio experts, model and talent agencies, and prop services. The book's distribution pattern fits accordingly.

A little more than 25 percent of each printing goes to art directors and creative directors at advertising agencies. One book will be used by more than one of these creative personnel.

The next 25 percent of the printing goes to film and video production houses, while 15 percent of the printing is given to model and talent agencies. Twenty percent finds its way to the studio of photographers and illustrators, 5 percent to equipment and service houses, and 4 percent to editors and publishers. The final part of the distribution is to bookstores, schools, libraries, and advertisers.

"When a photographer who wants to advertise calls me, the first thing I do is send him a rate card and a copy of an ad, so he can get an idea what his money purchases," says Bhash Mazunder, one of the sales reps on staff at the *Madison Avenue Handbook*.

"Once he receives the rate card, I'll give him a call and see how we could fit an ad into his promotional budget."

The photographer who decides to advertise in this publication has two choices. He can buy a color or black-and-white page, or a bold-face listing in the listings section. The bold-face listings start at $75 for two lines and go up from there. A typical listing might include the photographer's name, address, phone number, the name of his rep, and perhaps something unique like, "See our *Creative Black Book* page, advertising our services in the still-life area of commercial photography." Essentially, the bold-face listing becomes an advertisement for a directory page in another publication.

Like *Advertising Photography In Chicago*, you can also be listed in regular type *free of charge*. Simply send in your request on letterhead. Your listing will appear in the section of the book that corresponds to your location, because the *Madison Avenue Handbook* has listings grouped by geographic regions.

If you decide to purchase a directory page, the procedure might go something like this:

"The photographer will either come into our offices or I'll go to his studio," says Mazunder. "If I see a suggestion that I can make regarding the types of slides to use in the ad, I will. I'll also put him in touch with our art director or Peter Glenn, the publisher, who can help in the selection of images. If the photographer has already decided, or if he already has color separations made, I respect his decision."

There's a separate fee that covers the cost of layout and separations, which is approximately $100 to $250 for each color image used in the ad. The printing is done in the United States and the photographer gets one proof on which to make corrections before it goes back for the final printing. The actual costs of the ads follow later in this chapter. However, APA and ASMP members, take note. You get a special discount.

In analyzing whether or not to buy a directory page in the *Madison Avenue Handbook*, you should take into consideration its layout and marketing. That is, the book is not just for photographers. In fact, the bulk of the listings are not from photographers. They are from professionals in the other areas listed. The previously outlined distribution pattern corresponds, so that only a little more than 25 percent of the copies go to art and creative directors, the people who hire photographers for jobs.

What all this means is that the *Madison Avenue Handbook* isn't the greatest place to buy a full-page color or black-and-white ad. What's the point in advertising here if you can't fully reach the audience that can hire you for jobs? In fact, the publication acknowledges that its comprehensive listing of prop houses (animal rentals are also included in this category) is where it really stands out from the other directories.

Rather than buying a directory page, buy a bold-face listing and use it to plug your directory page in another publication. The cost is a lot less than buying the full-page ad, which will free up your money for other promotional efforts. Following is a list of directories you can advertise in that art directors, art buyers and others use to find photographers with whom they wish to do business. Contact each publication for specific deadlines for submission of ads. (Costs are current as of this writing and subject to change.)

The rate that you are charged should also include a certain amount of reprint pages. These reprints are reproductions of your ad, exactly as they appear in the directory, on the same stock and can be sent out to prospective clients as part of a direct mail promotion. They can also be used as part of your portfolio, to show a prospective client who hasn't seen your ad what the photographs look like in print.

Don't overlook the importance of reprints. They are a valuable promotional tool. If you have to decide between two directories that reach the same group of people you're after, and costs are equal, choose the one that gives you more reprints. Even if one charges a little more than the other, but gives you appreciably more reprints, the extra cost will be worth the promotional value that the reprints provide later on.

NATIONAL DIRECTORIES

THE CREATIVE BLACK BOOK
401 Park Avenue South
New York, NY 10016
(212) 684-4255

Contact Linda Kaufman, sales manager

Cost: A full page of color is $5,880; a color spread is $10,650; a full page of black and white is $3,850; a black-and-white spread is $6,930. The production charges range from $130 to $175. Page size is 6¼ × 10¾ inches.

The Creative Black Book *provides 2,000 reprints free if all materials, including mechanicals and art work, are in by a special reprint deadline. If you can't make the deadline (call ahead to find out what it is), it'll cost you $450 per color page (less for a black-and-white page) for each reprint page.*

The total number of copies printed is 40,000. Breakdown is as follows. There is free distribution to 20,500 art buyers, television producers, art directors, copy supervisors, and creative group supervisors in all North American and European advertising agencies that bill over five million dollars per annum. Paid distribution of 19,500 copies is to publications, corporate advertising and promotion personnel, designers, small advertising agencies, and other creative individuals.

MADISON AVENUE HANDBOOK
Peter Glenn Publications
17 East 48th Street
New York, NY 10017
(800) 223-1254

Contact Peter Glenn, editor and publisher

Cost: A full page of color costs $3,000; a full page of black and white, $1,950. Each color separation is $200 and up, depending on the *complexity of the job. Also, there's a 10-percent space discount in cases when the photographer provides color separations in accordance with the publisher's specifications. The page size is 5½ × 8 inches.*

The Madison Avenue Handbook *provides color advertisers with 500 reprints, provided they receive request for same within 45 days prior to going to press. Black-and-white reprints are also available on request.*

The total number of copies printed is 23,500. Breakdown is as follows. The first 10,575 copies are sent to ad agencies, corporations, and production houses. The remaining 12,925 copies go to other distribution sources, including bookstores and mail order sales.

AMERICAN PHOTOGRAPHY SHOWCASE

American Showcase
724 Fifth Avenue
New York, NY 10019
(212) 245-0981

Contact publisher, Ira Shapiro

Cost: A full page of color averages $3,200, while a custom-designed color page averages $3,500. A full page of black and white averages $2,675, while a full page of black and white that's custom designed is $2,950. Custom-designed pages feature full-bleed ads, with the photographer's logo, type, and design. The photographer provides the mechanical and any other camera-ready art.

The cost of a standard page includes the mechanical, typesetting, and one separation, which the printer retains. Each additional color photograph is $115. Each additional black-and-white photograph is $75.

The standard page ads are placed in alphabetical order, according to geographic region. The custom-designed page ads are given preferential treatment and put at the front of each geographic section. Page size is 9¼ × 11¾ inches, and there's a 10-percent discount if space is reserved by a specific deadline.

Photography Showcase *provides 2,000 free reprints. Circulation of this publication in the United States and Canada is a minimum of 40,000 copies, with distribution as follows. The first 17,000 copies are sent free to ad directors, art buyers, and others who hire photographers. Paid distribution of 23,000 is to retail outlets and others interested in seeing the advertisers' photographs.*

THE ASMP BOOK

Annuals Publishing Company
10 East 23rd Street
New York, NY 10010
(212) 475-1620

Contact publisher, Tad Crawford

In order to advertise in this directory, you must be a member of the American Society of Magazine Photographers, so membership cost should also be included in your promotion budget. Membership information is available from: Executive Director, ASMP, 205 Lexington Avenue, New York, NY 10016.

Cost: A full page of color ranges from $1,950 to $2,200, with the actual cost depending on the deadline the photographer meets. The first color separation is free and each additional one costs $100. A full page of black and white ranges from $1,950–2,200, with this cost also dependent upon the deadline the photographer meets. The first black-and-white photograph is free and each additional one costs $50. The page size was 7 × 9 inches in 1986, and it's supposed to increase in the future. The ASMP Book *provides all advertisers with 2,000 free reprints.*

The total number of copies printed is 30,000. Distribution is as follows. The first 16,000 copies are sent free-of-charge to design firms, advertising agencies, specific in-house advertising groups, multi-national corporations, and publishers. Also, outside of New York City, the four sections comprising The ASMP Book *are reprinted as a local publication and sent to corporations in each area.*

ADWEEK PORTFOLIO OF PHOTOGRAPHY

514 Shatto Place
Los Angeles, CA 90020
(213) 384-7100

Contact director of sales, Lynn Scanlon-Wagner

Cost: A full page of color costs $3,500. Price also includes one page *of copy. Two spreads of color, comprised of one page of copy and three pages of color photographs, is $9,000. The first color separation is free and there's a charge of $100 for each additional one. A full page of black and white is $2,800, and comes with an additional page of copy.*

There's a 10-percent discount for members of various professional organizations and return advertisers. Also, this publication is actually divided up into five portfolio editions: Graphic Design Photography, Creative Services Directory, Illustration, and Commercial Production. Regional advertising rates are available at discounted rates for the east, west, midwest, and south. Page size is 8⅝ × 10⅞ inches. With each spread purchased, 2,500 reprints are provided free.

The total number of copies printed is 55,000. Distribution is as follows. The first 25,000 copies are sent free of charge to corporations, advertising agencies, and design companies. The remaining 30,000 copies go to other distribution sources.

REGIONAL DIRECTORIES

ADVERTISING PHOTOGRAPHY IN CHICAGO

Alexander Communications, Inc.
212 W. Superior, Suite 400
Chicago, IL 60610
(312) 944-5155

Contact publisher, Paul Casper

Photographers advertising in this directory must work in Chicago or have a representative there.

Cost: A full page of color is $1,800. Included in the price is one page of copy free, on the left-hand side of the spread. The first color separation is free, each additional costs $125. A full page of black and white is $1,700. The price includes one page of copy, on the left-hand side of the spread. The first black-and-white halftone is free and each additional one costs $75. Page size is 7 × 9½ inches and 1,000 reprints are provided free.

The total circulation is 10,000. Copies are distributed free to qualified photography buyers both in this country and abroad. Breakdown is as follows. In the United States, 60 percent to the east and north central regions; 16 percent to the mid-atlantic region; 5 percent to the northeast; and 19 percent elsewhere.

CHICAGO CREATIVE DIRECTORY

333 North Michigan Avenue
Suite 810
Chicago, IL 60601
(312) 236-7337

Contact sales manager, Kurt Hansen

Cost: A full page of color is $1,350, when separations are provided by the advertiser. If not, a full page of color plus one separation is $2,150. Additional separations are provided at cost. A full page of black and white is $1,000, and the photographer provides the *mechanical and other camera-ready art. Page size is 5½ × 8½ inches and 1,000 free reprints are provided.*

The total number of copies printed is 10,000. The distribution is free, and saturates the Chicago market, including prominent ad agencies. It is also sent to art buyers and creative directors at ad agencies in ten other states that bill over $1 million, and nationally and in Canada to ad agencies that bill over $5,000,000.

CHICAGO TALENT SOURCEBOOK

212 W. Superior
Suite 400
Chicago IL 60610
(312) 944-5115

Contact publisher, Paul Casper

To advertise in this directory, you must work in Chicago or have a representative there.

Cost: A full page of color averages $2,025, with the price depending on the deadline you meet for ad submission. One color separation is provided free and each additional one costs $125.

A page of black and white averages $1,500 and the price depends upon the deadline the photographer meets for ad submission. Price includes one free black-and-white shot, with each additional one costing $75. Page size is 8½ × 11 inches. If the ad submission deadline is met, 1,000 reprints are provided free. If not, you pay $250 for 1,000 reprints.

A total of 10,000 copies are printed, most of which are distributed free to qualified art users and buyers nationally.

DESIGNSOURCE

Turnbull & Co.
19 Mount Auburn Street
Cambridge, MA 02138
(617) 864-1110

Contact editor, John I. Greely

Cost: A full page of color averages $1,345, depending upon the *deadline for ad submission the photographer meets. The first color separation is free and each additional one costs $120.*

A full page of black and white averages $1,175, depending upon the deadline for ad submission the photographer meets. The first black-and-white photograph is free and each additional one costs $50. The page size is 5⅛ × 8⅛ inches, with 1,000 reprints provided free.

A total of 10,000 copies are printed, which are distributed free to top personnel in design studios, advertising agencies, and publishing and in-house art departments in New England.

THE REGIONAL REVIEW SOURCE BOOKS

Dynamic Publications
901 Bonifant Road
Silver Spring, MD 20904
(800) 255-1777

Contact the executive secretary, James Pearson

Cost: A full page of color is $1,250, with an additional $137 for each separation. A full page of black and white is $1,250, with an additional cost of $75 per black-and-white photo. The page size is 5¼ × 10½ inches. Advertisers get 500 to 1,500 reprints, depending on the deal the photographer negotiates with the publication.

A total of 60,366 copies are printed. There are six different reviews, each one containing different listings keyed to the geographic location of advertisers. Breakdown is as follows. The Northern Review: *13,100 in the Midwest and New York State.* The Western Review: *12,282 in Chicago, the west, and New York.* The Southwest Review: *10,062 in Los Angeles, Chicago, New York, and the southwest.* The New York/New England Review: *12,980 in the New England states, New York, Los Angeles, and Chicago.* The Mid-Atlantic Review: *11,942 distributed from Florida to Pennsylvania, as well as Atlanta, Dallas, Chicago, Los Angeles, and New York.* The Canadian Review: *7,000 in Canada, New York, Chicago, and Los Angeles.*

A full set of these regional publications is sent to major art buyers throughout the United States. A mailing list of these art buyers is also supplied to advertising photographers.

SOUTHEAST CREATIVE DIRECTORY

802 Stovall Boulevard NE
Atlanta, GA 30342
(404) 261-7599

Contact sales manager, Sherisse McLaurin

Cost: A full page of color is $1,300 when separations are provided by the photographer, and $2,100 when the publisher supplies one separation. Other charges for color are available upon request.

A full page of black and white is $950 and the photographer provides the mechanical and other camera-ready art. Other production charges for black and white are available upon request. The page size is 4½ × 7½ inches. Advertisers get 500 free reprints.

A total of 10,000 copies are printed, of which 7,000 copies are distributed to advertising agencies billing over $1,000,000 in a 10-state area covering the southeast. The other 3,000 copies are sent nationally to agencies with billings over $5,000,000.

THE WORKBOOK

940 North Highland
Los Angeles, CA 90038
(213) 856-0008

Contact the publisher, Alexis Scott

Only open to photographers with studios or reps in California.

Cost: A full page of color averages $2,588, depending upon the deadline for ad submission that the photographer meets. There's an additional charge of $100 per separation.

A page of black and white averages $1,738, depending upon the deadline for ad submission that the photographer meets. There's an additional charge of $50 for each black-and-white halftone. The page size is 8½ × 11 inches, with 1,000 reprints provided free.

The total number of copies printed is 27,000. Distribution is as follows. The first 15,000 copies go to every major in-house art department, ad agency, and design studio across the country; 5,600 copies are distributed in other countries; and 6,000 are sold in United States retail markets. A corporate list is also available to advertisers.

FLYERS, MAILERS, AND BROCHURES

These promotional pieces fall into the category of direct-mail materials or are directly distributed by the photographer. Their use depends on the type of work you do and the amount of money you want to spend.

For any of these pieces, you'll have to supply all the materials for a printer to produce the piece, including copy, artwork, and mechanicals. You'll also have to explain your needs to the printer you choose. While flyers are relatively simple to produce, you will be well-advised to work with a promotion specialist on mailers and brochures unless you have a background in the graphic arts.

No matter what type of mailing you choose to send, it would be wise to investigate obtaining a bulk-mail permit from your local post office. If you're thinking of doing any kind of quantity mailing, the costs can add up quickly. A bulk-mail permit can often cut these costs in half.

Flyers

Flyers are the least expensive form of paid promotion available to the photographer. The cheapest way to have them printed is to do the layout yourself on a sheet of paper, sticking down the various elements with rubber cement. These elements might include your logo, a picture from a recent job, and copy explaining your service.

It's a simple matter then to take this camera-ready art to a local printer and have him make the copies on a Xerox machine. The higher the quantity you have printed, the less the cost. For example, if you print up 200 flyers from the same camera-ready art, it should not cost you more than five cents a copy, or ten dollars for the whole job.

As discussed earlier, you can use these flyers as "handouts," distributing them locally in your area, or you can send them to a more specific clientele. The wedding and portrait photographer would go through his files and compile "list A," which would contain the names and addresses of former clients. He then makes up "list B," which contains the names and addresses of prospective clients. The latter is formed from references and engagement announcements published in newspapers. The two lists are compiled onto one master list. Each person or persons listed is sent a flyer that outlines the photographer's services. If the photographer is really aggressive, he can follow up the mailing in two weeks with a phone call to each name on the list to see if the promotion has worked.

Mailers

This type of promotional piece can be as simple as a printed postcard with a single photograph, a reprint of your directory-page ad, or a full-blown, professionally designed campaign involving a series of cards.

Here's an example of how photographer Ronn Orenstein worked with designer Kimberly Prezyna to produce a distinctive, multipurpose mailer.

"Ronn shoots a lot of things," says Prezyna. "What I decided to do was specialize in one specific type of image."

Orenstein had done a series of self-assigned photographs involving beverages and they were what Prezyna chose to feature. She created a 5 × 7-inch mount made out of black-linen stock. She then had the photographer's logo printed in gold, silk-screened lettering. The central eye-grabber was an area ruled in silk-screened gold, which could contain one photograph measuring 4 × 5 inches. Finally, Prezyna added a vellum overlay and had Orenstein's name silk-screened across it in gold.

The completed card can only be described as elegant. The kicker is that Prezyna designed the card so that it can contain any 4 × 5-inch C-print that Orenstein chooses to insert in the future.

Because printing costs are variable, it's difficult to list average costs for mailers. Prices will vary not only according to how deluxe you want the mailer to be, but will also change depending on the area of the country you live in. The best thing to do is check with a printer in your area and ask him for an estimate of cost, making sure he has the capability to do the job you have in mind.

As a rough guideline, Serbin Communications, Inc., the publishers of *Photographer's Forum* magazine, is now offering four-color printing services that are affordable on even the tightest of promotional budgets. For $585, which includes up to six separations of color photographs, they will print your choice of the following:

2,500 9 × 12-inch directory-type pages
2,500 6 × 9-inch cards
5,000 4½ × 6-inch cards

For any of these pieces, you have to supply the layout. Still, $585 is a hard price to beat for the amount of material you'll be getting.

Brochures

Certainly the most deluxe form of mailer, brochures are becoming increasingly popular as really stand-out promotional pieces. Because of the expense involved in this type of promotion, to squander funds on an ineffective brochure would be foolish. Unless you have a strong sense of promotion and design, it would be best to turn the development of a brochure over to a professional consultant and designer.

However, Chicago photographer Dennis Manarchy is one who has successfully created a truly spectacular brochure on his own. Manarchy started out with the lyrics from a song by rock group Dire Straits entitled "Private Investigations." He liked the lyrics and decided to use them as a thematic guide to the images he would put into his promotional brochure.

Manarchy got permission to reproduce the song title and lyrics in his brochure, and then selected his images to conform to the basic idea. The concept became a rock video on paper and the result was a 38-page brochure that was sent to clients and prospective clients.

When it actually came time for delivery, Manarchy continued the "Private Investigations" theme. He and members of his staff printed the names of the brochure recipients on envelopes labeled "Top Secret." They were subsequently hand-delivered, with the added touch of a fresh red rose.

CATALOGS

Similar to brochures, catalogs are among the deluxe items you can add to your campaign program. However, these carry the extra benefit of having the client share in the cost of production, as well as being excellent examples of how a photographer can actually work with a product.

Catalogs are produced in conjunction with a store or manufacturer of a specific item. As part of the photographer's fee for shooting the job, reprints of the catalog are provided for his own promotional use. If the catalog is well-produced, this type of promotion can be quite prestigious.

Here's an example of how one photographer successfully used a catalog. "Artwear" is a store in New York City's trendy Soho district that specializes in selling jewelry as art; that is, jewelry of innovative and exceptional design. When the store decided to produce a catalog featuring the creations that it sells, the store's founder and owner, Robert Lee Morris, collaborated on the production of a catalog with fashion photographer Klaus Laubmayer.

What they produced was a combination of Morris's understanding of the jewelry, plus Laubmayer's artistic photographs, which accurately rendered the emotional feeling Morris wanted the jewelry to convey. The result was a handsome, 60-page catalog, which both Artwear and Laubmayer used as a promotional piece. Artwear sent the catalog to a select group of clients who purchase the expensive works; Laubmayer did his mailing to members of the New York fashion press, from whom he received a lot of publicity. Laubmayer subsequently received several offers to shoot work for various clients. He was also able to sell some of the photographs taken for the catalog to *Stern*, the West German magazine.

CALENDARS AND POSTERS

These two forms of promotion are among the most prestigious—and therefore, most expensive—types of effort. The rule of thumb here is excellence in every phase of production, beginning with the photography and design, and ending with high-quality production.

If done correctly, a calendar or poster can be the most successful type of promotion you can create. What you're attempting to gain here is that most prized possession: a spot on an art director's or art buyer's wall. There, your work will not only be seen constantly by that recipient, but everyone else who enters his or her office. Some of these efforts become so popular that they are requested by other art buyers who didn't receive one first time around.

Let's take a look at two photographers who have used these types of promotion with great success.

Bruce Bennett is a Long Island-based commercial photographer. He also happens to be the official photographer for the New York Islanders hockey team. Every year, he sends out a calendar with each month illustrated by a shot of the Islanders in action.

"We had a casino that was willing to sponsor the calendar, with the Islanders publishing it." Bennett recalls. "While the Islanders have the right to use my photographs in any of their publications, the calendar was a gray area. However, I told the team owners they could use the photos in the calendar, as long as they gave me enough to send to my clients. The total press run is 20,000 and the team gives them out to the fans during the first game of the season."

With his calendar, Bennett is confirming in people's minds, especially those of prospective clients, that he is a great photographer, associated with one of the most successful sports franchises in modern history. The inherent message is that if the New York Islanders have confidence in his ability, then you can too. It's a tough argument to contradict.

New York photographer William Coupon created a minor stir among the advertising community when he published his first promotional poster. Coupon gathered 56 color photographs of the famous—and not-so-famous—people he had photographed, and had them all printed together, side-by-side, on one poster. This myriad of faces included such diverse personalities as performance artist Laurie Anderson, Olympic diver Greg Louganis, astronaut-turned-politician John Glenn, and actor Dustin Hoffman.

In addition to being entertaining, well-designed, and exquisitely printed, the subtle message behind Coupon's poster is that he is capable of photographing all kinds of people, including some of the most famous in the world. Therefore, he is also capable of taking on the client's assignment.

The promotion worked. After sending the poster to advertising agencies, magazines, and photo galleries, Coupon hit pay dirt.

"I'm getting advertising work as a result of the poster, gallery shows too," he reveals. In fact, the poster was so successful that Coupon is producing two more.

"It took me months to design them," Coupon says. "One poster is a single, black-and-white portrait of the 'Talking Heads' ' David Byrne. The other is a series of 14 environmental portraits. I also expect to do more posters in the future.

"With these efforts, I'm going for a long-term effect. They're for all time, not just typical stuff. I get calls for them every day. They educate people as to the style of photography I do."

It's hard to predict what the long-term effect of Coupon's posters will be, but if it's anything like the short-term, he'll be promoting himself into more and more jobs.

THE ELITE

I've said that brochures, catalogs, calendars, and posters are the most prestigious paid promotional items. They're the top of the line, and as such, very expensive to produce.

Smart photographers are always looking for a way to subsidize their efforts and you can too—by seeking out the right kind of support.

Paper manufacturers, such as Mead and Westvaco, are known for running advertisements for their products featuring the work of excellent photographers. The point of the ads is to show how well such work can be reproduced on their paper. Many times these campaigns are backed up by brochures sent directly to clients. Having your photography chosen for inclusion in one of these advertisements not only ensures you the finest printing quality available, but as a bonus, these ads are often run in such publications as *Communication Arts* and *Photo/Design*, which are read by art directors and other art buyers. You, in turn, can get reprints of the ad or brochure to send out on your own.

Granted, this type of campaign is only available to the few, but you can just as easily work with your printer on a similar basis.

"One of the best ways to cut costs is to make a deal with the printer." says designer Kimberly Prezyna. "In exchange for the printer's credit on your calendar, poster, or other promotional piece, the printer agrees to do the job at either a considerable discount or *gratis*." Sometimes, the job is done for free when the printer is using the same printing process for a paid job and throws your promotion on at the end of the print run.

This saves the printer money. He doesn't have to design his own promotional piece. He uses the piece he's printing up for the photographer to promote his printing business.

As to the costs of unsubsidized efforts, the rule is that the larger your print run, the cheaper the cost of the overall job. Printing in bulk saves money. However, as Kimberly Prezyna says, how much a printer charges for a job varies widely and it's impossible to generalize.

"I've found that when you call printers A, B, and C for the same job, they give you prices at different ends of the spectrum. The best thing to do is comparison shop and go with the printer who doesn't say 'yes, yes, yes,' but who really knows what you're talking about and can meet your needs.

"Bear in mind," Prezyna continues, "that certain printing processes, regardless of where you go, cost additional. Something embossed (such as type) will cost more than something flat. Something that's hot stamped (a simulated engraving process) in a gold color, is more expensive than using gold ink flat on a page. Everything adds up. Varnishing adds more money, as does a printing element that's die cast, such as a folder that's cut a certain way."

In other words, when budgeting out your promotion—any kind of promotion—keep in mind that *everything* costs extra.

PROMOTING YOUR PROMOTIONS

While I'm on the subject of the costs of paid promotions, this seems the perfect time to mention ways to get the most from the money you've spent, that is, how to promote your promotion. The fact is that as the field of promotion grows, it produces some fine examples of creative work, many of which are becoming judged on their own merits.

There are currently a number of awards annuals published which contain categories such as best self-promotional piece, best photography used in a single ad, best campaign, and other similar areas, depending on the annual to which you submit your work.

Because these publications are heavily distributed to art buyers, art directors, and creative directors at ad agencies, they provide the winning photographers with instant credibility and a forum for their work. Such exposure can definitely lead to jobs.

Two of the most prestigious award books are the *Creativity* annual put out by Art Direction Book Company, which also publishes *Art Direction* magazine and the *Photography Annual* published by *Communication Arts* magazine.

The *Photography Annual* awards "bests" in the following areas: advertising, including single ads, record jackets and other forms of packaging; a campaign of five ads or less; book cover jackets; editorial; work-for-sale (such as posters); institutional (annual reports and catalogs); and self-promotion. To enter the competition for the *Photography Annual*, you may write for an entry form to: Communication Arts, P.O. Box 10300, Palo Alto CA 94303.

The *Creativity* annuals, which also go to creative personnel at ad agencies, have similar categories that photographers may enter. To get an application, write to: Art Direction—Creativity, 10 East 39 St., New York NY 10016.

Nikon, Inc. and *Photo District News* are also co-sponsoring their own annual awards, called *Photo District News/Nikon Self- Promotion Awards*. Categories include best ongoing campaign, consisting of four or more related pieces distributed over a period of six to eighteen months; print placements, including self-promotion ads of one page or more that appeared in creative directories, annuals, or magazines; and direct mail, including cards, mailers, posters, and other printed pieces. For more information and an application, write: PDN/Nikon Self-Promotion Awards, Photo District News, 49 East 21 St., New York NY 10010.

SPECIALIZED PAID PROMOTIONS

Photographers should always keep an eye open for any opportunity to promote themselves. This often goes beyond the standard type of promotions I've discussed here. One of the most popular specialized promotion times is the holiday season. Many photographers see Christmas not just as a time of cheer, but a prime time to promote their services.

A successful holiday promotion not only gives the photographer a chance to thank the client for work in the past, it will also make a client or prospective client think about the photographer all year and, hopefully, give him more work in the future.

Calendars and date books are very popular holiday items, but people/illustration photographer Jack Reznicki goes for the more creative at this time of the year.

"My Christmas promotions are non-photographic and are sent to clients and prospective clients," Reznicki says. "In 1983, I gave out a red cookie tin, which contained home-baked, chocolate-chip cookies that my rep baked in her kitchen.

"On top of the tin was my logo, which I consider to be distinctive—it's my last name spelled out phonetically, with the words, 'Just call me Jack' underneath in small letters.

"For my 1984 promotion, I gave away hand-made Jack-in-the-boxes as a humorous play on my name. And for Christmas, 1985, I gave out a one-quart container of cider. The label had a picture of my rep and myself posed in American Gothic style clothing and the words 'Reznicki Vineyards' underneath."

Reznicki makes sure that any promotion, whether done during Christmas or any time of year, be followed up by a phone call to the recipients.

"I think it's hard to track promotions," Reznicki adds. "For instance, I got one Job from Wrangler because an art director saw my rep and portfolio and a few weeks later saw my ad in the *Creative Black Book*. What got me the job? The ad or my rep going up *previously* with the portfolio?

"When I send out a mailer, I look for a response rate. It's measured by this simple question: Is my book getting called up more since the promotion has been out there?"

So far, Reznicki's promotions are working.

Another photographer who's creative with his promotions all year 'round is Bruce Bennett, the previously mentioned photographer for the New York Islanders hockey team.

While Bennett is best-known for his work for the Islanders, he does a lot of other types of photography as well, including commercial and editorial work. But Bennett found that being based on Long Island, some potential clients thought of him as "small potatoes."

To counter this misconception, Bennett took a booth at the Long Island Trade Show, which is attended by the advertising and public relations community on Long Island—the market that Bennett wanted to hit. Bennett takes up the story.

"The booth was plastered with laminated shots showing what I'd done: sports action, product, editorial, and advertising. I had a video running with interviews I had done on the syndicated TV show, 'World of Photography,' cable TV shows on Long Island, and spots in between periods of Islander games."

But videos and laminated photographs are fairly standard promotional items.

"I had to find some way to stand out from the crowd and give people an image to stick in their head." He found it.

"I decorated the booth with Mr. Potato Head toys and sacks of potatoes. There was a banner on the booth that said, 'Just Because We're From Long Island Doesn't Mean We're Small Potatoes.'

"People came up to the booth and kept asking, 'What are the potatoes for?' When they left, they got a Mr. Potato Head and a promotional piece that contained the tag line on the banner."

Subsequently, Bennett sent the Mr. Potato Head promotion to prospective and current clients for Christmas. A total of 4,000 were sent out, including Ms. Potato Heads to female clients, as a non-chauvinistic gesture. As to results, he says:

"We made our money back on the promotion in terms of additional work, but what the long term results will be, I don't know.

"From college courses I took in marketing, I know that you can't hit them once and let it go. You have to follow up each promotional piece with phone calls and then another promotion.

"Right now, we're working on a two-pronged attack. We're still sending out the potato promo and we're working on a promotional piece involving ducks; ducks and potatoes both being symbols of Long Island."

Another of Bennett's creative promotions, initially given out during Christmas, was a T-shirt. It had three red bullet holes on it and the copy, "I got shot at Bruce Bennett Studios."

"It got a great reaction," Bennett recalls. "Some clients got the shirts that were 50/50 cotton/polyester. Some got ones made in Pakistan."

Want to take a wild guess which clients got the better made shirt? In fact, Bennett is very pragmatic about his promotions.

"I get calls from former clients saying, 'Hey, I didn't get the Islander calendar.' I say, 'Hey, I didn't get the work!' "

WORKING WITH PROFESSIONALS

I've spent much of this chapter hinting at the idea of hiring the services of a professional designer to aid in the creation of a successful promotion. If you're creative in your own right, or have a background in graphic design, you can do much of the work described here on your own.

However, if you've read through all this information and still don't have a clue of where to begin, you might be well advised to seek the input of a professional promotion consultant or a graphic designer.

What Does a Graphic Designer Do?

Kimberly Prezyna, who has been quoted previously, is a professional graphic designer who specializes in designing promotions for photographers, but she didn't start out that way.

"I tried to fit into the corporate structure," she says, "but it didn't work. I'd worked for Pennysaver and Fairchild Publications. It was at Fairchild that I finally decided to go out on my own.

"I wanted to get into the photography industry. So, I went to a photo industry head hunter who sent me to Duggal Color labs as a counter girl. Later, I worked at another lab, where I did everything but feed film."

Sounds like good experience.

"Yes, but the paycheck started to bounce, so I went to another lab called Colorite. That's where I started discussing with photographers what their promotional efforts were. They would bring in mechanicals for brochures and mailers that weren't even the proper size.

"I began to question why there weren't specialists who could help photographers design their visual pieces. That's when I decided to get into advertising art and design myself. Becoming a graphic designer who specialized in working with photographers on visual promotions was a way to do just that. I would become a designer for photographers."

Prezyna points out that photographers are wonderfully creative people who don't necessarily have the perspective to promote their art. Says Prezyna:

"I can go in a studio and crop a bad chrome and make it look beautiful for a promotional piece, because I have perspective, where the photographer might not."

She also believes that the limits on promotion are simply the limits on the designer's and the photographer's imaginations.

"What's most important is designing a promotional piece that isn't like all the rest," she adds.

Prezyna begins a promotion project by first consulting with a photographer who's interested in employing her. She'll show the photographer her portfolio and then discuss ideas for a promotion that's specially tailored to the photographer's needs.

"If it's a photographer who specializes in still lifes, for example, we need a direction in the promotion that stresses this fact. I try to get as specific as possible, like the mailer I designed for Ronn Orenstein."

Perhaps her most unusual promotion was for a photographer named Darwin Davidson. Davidson specializes in shooting interiors, exteriors, and furnishings. In Prezyna's opinion, "He had never done any quality self-promotion work."

After conferring with Davidson, she decided to work with a play on the words "Darwin's Theory," using a direct reference to Charles Darwin's "Theory of Evolution." This provided a theme for the campaign that would hopefully stay in the minds of prospective clients.

Davidson had hired Prezyna to create the copy as well as the design for the promotion. So, before going any further, she went to her thesaurus and eventually came up with the key phrases, Darwin's Theory of Interpretation" and "Theory Becomes Fact." These would form the core of the promotion's copy.

The actual promotional piece, a brochure, measured a foldable 12 × 9 inches, with three images on the inside that corresponded to Darwin's photographic strengths—interiors, exteriors, and furnishings. Two logos were used and sandwiched between them was the copy. On the last page is Darwin's logo, his name, address, phone number, a list of ten of his most well-known clients, and Prezyna's design credit.

"Generally, I don't like to be involved in the printing after the piece has been designed. But printers can endanger my reputation (and spoil the job) by not following my printing instructions and using different inks on paper stocks than the ones I've indicated. That's why I'm finding, more and more, that I am going to have to get involved so things don't get messed up. When I take this active a role in printing, my fee is 20 percent of the actual printing cost.

"Also, I have to learn how to be price conscious. In this way, I can design pieces with materials that are affordable." Prezyna has some advice for photographers doing direct mail promotions.

"What I recommend is that you send out different pieces, brochures, mailers, whatever, four times a year, minimum. Hit them once a season. The idea is to make sure that your name isn't forgotten."

In commenting on her competition, she also points out a common problem photographers have with promotion.

"My greatest competition is art directors. Usually, it's a friend of the photographer who advises him and then does the work on a barter arrangement. In other words, I'll design for you and in return, you shoot a job for me.

"My experience, though, with barters and trade-offs is that many times, one party feels slighted. You may have started out as friends but you end up as enemies, and what's more, you've blown a contact."

What a Full-Service Agency Can Do

When Maureen Nicoll was working as a photography editor for The Image Bank stock agency, she'd occasionally get together with Pauleen Augustine. Pauleen was the marketing and senior editor of the *ASMP Book*.

"We'd have portfolio consultations. Sometimes, we'd advise photographers on direct mail promotions and how to advertise in sourcebooks like the *Creative Black Book*," Maureen remembers.

Eventually, they left their respective jobs and formed a partnership in New York City. Their new firm is called PM Associates. It's a full-service agency that advises and helps photographers promote themselves in all areas of promotion.

"What we do initially is meet with a photographer for two-and-a-half hours and put them through a battery of 30 questions. They are designed to find out what his professional successes and failures are, how much he makes, how much he wants to make, and how best to achieve the goals he's set for himself. Once the questions are answered and we've gotten to know him a little better, we'll advise him on future promotional efforts," says Maureen. She continues:

"After the consult, we'll look at everything he's ever shot and redesign his portfolio so it's directed at the market he wants to either strengthen or get into. We'll also advise him on the proper mailing lists to use and how to approach potential clients. Then we follow up for three months, to see how he's doing."

Because of their backgrounds, Pauleen and Maureen have a lot of inside knowledge about how best to advertise in directories.

"Advertising depends on the photographer's specialty and where he's at in his career. Before you advertise, you should know who reads which sourcebook and how much of an audience it really delivers, so your advertising dollar is spent wisely.

"Some sourcebooks make their mailing lists available. With that mailing list you can target the market, which is what we advocate."

Once the directory is selected, they'll assist the photographer in culling images from their portfolio for the ad. They then turn to their graphic designers to lay out the page. Maureen finds that the biggest problem photographers encounter with their directory pages is the quality of images.

"What we're selling is photography," she points out. "We showcase photography. I've seen some beautifully designed pages, but the content was not up to par. The layout is not as important as the photographs."

Conversely, Maureen also mentions that you may be using great photographs, but the layout is so showy that it draws attention away from the shots. She cautions against this and tells her graphic designers that the photographs have to be given precedence.

In the area of direct mail promotions, advice is just as select. Photographers are advised on the basis of what their specialty is, at what point they are in their career and, of course, how much money they have to spend.

"You know, any photographer who spends a lot of money to send out 20,000 pieces for a mailing (brochures, mailers, or posters), and many do, is making a big mistake. With a promotion of this magnitude, the marketing is way off. I don't know any one market that is that large.

"Most markets for a promotional piece are usually not more than 500 people (art directors and other art buyers). The exceptions are when you're doing a promotion to reach a national audience. So you may be sending out thousands of pieces to various cities and regions around the country, in addition to hitting the market in your hometown."

In general, Maureen sees two big problems with photographers' promotional efforts: They don't target the audience and they don't do any follow-up.

"Photographers don't study the market or the market potential, because they are not the best business people. Once an ad goes in a magazine or a mailing goes out, they don't follow it up to see how successful the promotion is.

"There's the problem of peer pressure. They see a competitor advertising in a particular sourcebook and they figure they have to buy an ad too, even though it may be reaching the wrong market for their photographic specialty. Sometimes, our advice to a client is they'd be better off putting their money into a CD account than an indiscriminate, untracked, 'keeping up with the Jones' type of promotion.

"Then there's the issue of exposure. Too often, we'll hear a story from a photographer who indiscriminately advertised and got no new contacts on the basis of that ad. Their rationalization will be, 'At least the ad got me some exposure.'

"*The issue of exposure should not come up with a photographer who's well along into his career.* If you're already established, you don't have to tell people who you are. They already know who you are."

Maureen Nicoll's most salient piece of advice:

"Self-promotion doesn't get jobs. It's a hook to get your portfolio called in by the potential client. It's the portfolio that'll get you the work."

Of course, you have to be called in in the first place and that will depend on the success of your promotional efforts.

GOING WITH THE PROS

A graphic designer like Kimberly Prezyna or a full-service agency like PM Associates is your best choice in putting together a paid promotional effort. We've touched on the reasons why, but let's summarize them now: They're experts at what they do; they have the perspective in selecting your photographs; they take the promotional burden off your shoulders; they have easier access to resources, such as printers and other production suppliers.

Budgeting

Like any other area, the use of specialists costs. A graphic designer can charge anywhere from an average of $500 to $2,500 for his services, which can include camera-ready art, specifically the mechanical of the ad or promotional element that's ready to go to the printer.

At this writing, PM Associates was the only full-service agency that did portfolio reviews, evaluations, offers marketing suggestions, and promotional designs. The only figure they are willing to give out is that it costs $400 for the two-and-a-half hour portfolio consultation and review. After that, promotional efforts get rather specialized and Maureen declined to get specific about costs.

In general, the larger a firm is, the more money they'll charge you.

The lone guy, with a lower overhead and mark-up, will charge less in comparison for his services.

When choosing a firm or individual to work with you on paid promotions, use these four selection criteria:

1. Look at his or her portfolio. It should contain previous promotional efforts. If the designer doesn't have a portfolio to show you, forget it. He or she doesn't have the credentials to do the job.

2. You should have confidence in the designer's ability to do the job and do it on time.

3. You should be convinced that the designer gives 100 percent in doing the job.

4. Whatever services you're buying, they should be affordable so that you won't have to give up food until more money is pumped into the business.

Selecting a Graphic Designer

Once the decision has been made to hire a graphic designer, you have to select one. How to do it? The answer is the Graphic Artists Guild. Based in New York City, with nine chapters around the country, the Graphic Artists Guild is an organization composed of graphic artists. This organization runs a job referral service that might be very helpful to you.

"If you live in New York, or you want to work with a graphic artist based in New York, the easiest way to select one is to call the Guild's referral service," says Margi Trapani, Communications Director for the Graphic Artists Guild.

"The referral service is free to clients," she continues. "You call up and tell us what you need designed and what your budget is. What we will then do is put you in touch with two or three artists who meet your criteria for the job. We do that by contacting the artists directly and having them call you. Then, you can arrange to take a look at their portfolio.

"We hope that anyone using the referral service will follow standard business practices in their negotiations with the artist. An example where this might be a problem is if a client says that they want to employ an artist to create a work-for-hire. In such a case, we might have trouble finding someone to do the job."

That would be terribly ironic. Photographers, who for years have complained about doing work-for-hire jobs, should not try to impose that same crippling business agreement on a graphic designer.

"We don't get involved in negotiations," says Trapani, "unless there's a real ethical problem." In other words, within the limits of good business practices and common sense, you're free to negotiate the best deal possible.

If you want to take advantage of the referral service, you can call the Graphic Artists Guild referral service at (212) 677-6607. Or, you can write them at 30 East 20 Street, New York, NY 10003.

"You can also find graphic artists through their ads in the directories, like the *Creative Black Book*," Trapani advises, "though more illustrators advertise than graphic artists. If you're located out of New York City and you want to employ a graphic artist in your region of the country, you can contact one of our nine chapters directly."

While the individual chapters do not have a formal job referral service as the New York one does, they will try and put you in touch with a graphic artist who could do the job for you in the area that the chapter services. Here are the phone numbers for the other eight chapters of the Graphic Artists Guild: Atlanta (404) 262-8077; Boston (617) 451-5362; Los Angeles (213) 933-7199; Burlington, VT (802) 658-1379; Colorado (303) 443-5584; Indiana (317) 639-2787; Central Florida (813) 595-2275; Buffalo, NY (716) 837-3761.

"You may also try contacting freelance employment services in your vicinity. They may represent graphic artists," Trapani continues. "However, we can't vouch for their reliability. Of course, if you're having trouble finding a graphic artist, you can consult the Yellow Pages. You may come up with something."

A FEW WORDS FROM YOUR AUDIENCE

Perhaps the best people to offer advice on your promotion pieces are the people who receive them. Let's take a look at what a few of these recipients had to say about the promotions they receive—and what they'd like to receive from photographers.

ELIZABETH PRICE
Print Service Manager
Leo Burnett, Chicago

Elizabeth Price is a print service manager with the Leo Burnett advertising agency in Chicago. She is an art buyer—the person who negotiates for and then buys the images from the photographer or rep—and has additional duties in traffic and production.

She gets all kinds of promotional pieces in the mail, including calendars, posters, and mailers.

"I enjoy things like a still life on a black background that pops out at you, where the graphics as well as the colors are strong. I think that posters, in particular, are a good way to promote your photography.

"Of the photographers whose work comes across my desk, or who come up to show me their portfolios, I'll recommend the ones that impress me the most to the art director. But regardless of what I'm impressed with, it's the art director who's going to make the final call."

Price points out that art directors, in addition to receiving paid promotions, also page through the creative directories, looking at the ads and searching for talented photographers with whom they'd like to work.

"Still, art directors might be apprehensive to try someone new," Price points out. "That's one reason it's difficult to break in (to a new market). I've also heard of art directors who monitor the assistants to the heavy hitters, and then become independents themselves."

Once the art director narrows down his choices for a job, Price's expertise is once again employed.

"The art director will want bids, for example, from three different photographers for one job. I'll go out and get those bids. I work with a lot of accounts that don't have much money, so sometimes, it's the photographer who bids the least that gets the assignment. It's part of my job to see if a photographer can live with a little less money when the occasion demands." Price will also try, depending upon the complexity of the job the art director has envisioned, to occasionally spend a little more on the job.

Essentially, Price has to function as both connoisseur of photography and businesswoman. Her aesthetic appreciation of the work has to remain subservient to the economic demands of the job, while still producing an image that is not only affordable, but an artistic stand-out. Otherwise, the client will not be satisfied. As we all know, the client is all-important because it is that ephemeral entity that pays the bills.

Now, let's hear from two art directors who, despite working for the same agency, approach photographers and their promotions in a different manner.

CANDACE VAN STRYKER

Art Director
Young and Rubicam, New York City

Ms. Van Stryker is an art director with one of the most powerful advertising agencies in the world, Young and Rubicam. It's her job to work with photographers on ads for products that appear in print.

Over the course of a week, Van Stryker receives all kinds of paid promotions, though mailers seem to be the most popular. Would a mailer make her hire a photographer for a job?

"I usually never hire a photographer on the basis of a mailer," she says. "If a mailer really catches my eye, I might put it in my scrap folder for future consideration." She points out that rarely do photographers follow up the sending of mailers with a phone call.

"A lot of them just don't call," Van Stryker confirms. "Or they may call a few weeks after they sent it out and expect me to remember it." Why don't the mailers impress her more?

"A lot of photographers aren't that great. There are few who really know how to light and design a shot and that lack of knowledge

and ability is reflected in the stuff they send me. Some of it looks like I could take the shot if I had a bank of lights and reflectors." Does she ever get paid promotions that impress her? Van Stryker responds:

"A few years ago, a photographer sent me a poster that was really nice. I framed it and I look at it in the hallway every time I go up the stairs." If she liked the poster so much, why didn't she hire him?

"There was nothing I was doing that he'd fit into, so I never called his book in. There were other people I saw whose work was better." So, where does Van Stryker find the new photographers to work with? Not from their ads in the creative directories.

"The only time I look at the directories is if I need a visual representation of a concept I'm working on. I'll use it as an example of what I want." Van Stryker keeps these examples in her scrap folder.

"I just looked at my scrap folder and saw a picture by Charles Ford of a woman with her hair blowing that's nice, and a mailer from Steve Steigman that I kept." What does impress her enough to call a photographer's book in?

"I look through the awards books, at ads that won awards and see what catches my eye. If something does, I might call the photographer's book in, if the photographer's work is applicable to a job I'm working on at the time."

Her procedure for calling a book in is simple. She'll call the photographer or the photographer's rep and ask them to leave the book at her office at lunchtime, which is really the only time she has during a busy schedule to take a look at new work.

"Reps love the fact that I give them a quick reply. I should also mention that when I'm looking at a portfolio, I'm looking for a few specific things.

"First, how the photographer works through problems. Second, does he know how to light and do a great job? Third, his sense of graphic design."

The portfolios usually have mailers included. If Van Stryker likes the photographer's work but doesn't have a job for him immediately, she'll take the mailer and keep it on file, once again for future consideration.

"I'll look at anyone's portfolio," she points out. "I just looked at a Japanese photographer's portfolio, composed of self-assigned

work. I liked his sense of design and I could see the way he worked through problems. I'll keep him in mind should a job come up that I think he fits.

"That's the way I work. When I have an assignment, I think of the way it should be shot. Then I think of the photographer who'd be perfect to shoot that particular job."

Like Chicago's Elizabeth Price, Van Stryker also has to be aware of monetary considerations. She wants to get the most for the money. A photographer who hasn't broken into the big-time yet might be a little more willing to negotiate when it comes time to discuss fees.

Van Stryker's overall feeling is that the quality of photographers' work, as represented by the various types of paid promotions I've discussed and the portfolio itself, is quite poor. Whether or not this is true is not the point. If you're really doing quality work, here's one art director who'd like to see what you're doing.

GUY MIGLIACCIO

Art Director
Young and Rubicam, New York City

Guy Migliaccio's goal is that each ad that he designs stand on its own.

"I like each one to have a certain style, so they don't all look alike. Each photographer's style of lighting is like fingerprints, varied and distinctive. That's why I like to work with a number of different photographers." But Migliaccio does not look at paid promotions initially as a source for good photographers.

"A promotion says to me that this photographer is a stable individual, who's also successful enough to spend money on promotional material. A successful promotion should make you aware of the person. A one-shot deal is a waste of money. Remind me you're there with a promotional schedule that's carefully thought out.

"The ones that fail do so because they're not well thought out." Migliaccio continues. "I might get a 5 × 7-inch mailer that's a pretty picture, but so what? As opposed to taking that shot one step further,

like incorporating it as part of a calendar that might stick around my office for a while. Overall, I like to see an idea behind it.

"There's this one guy, whose last name begins with a 'Z.' He regularly sends me promotional cards, all different sizes, that are covered by a gauzy white cloth. On the cloth in white Helvetica type, is his initial. I like that. I'd call him in if I needed him. I think photographers need an intelligent 'schtick' like that to catch an art director's eye."

Another promotion that caught Migliaccio's eye was photographer Michael Geiger's fold-out mailer. Each image in the mailer was "... stunning and powerful. But I won't send for a portfolio unless I have something in the works, especially if I want a different look. I like to work with photographers who can give me input to an idea I've already thought out and bring something extra to the job. They may have an idea I don't. It leaves room for improvement."

Migliaccio has a drawer in his office where he keeps all the paid promotions that he likes. Periodically, he whittles it down and sometimes, he'll go to the drawer to choose a photographer.

Migliaccio doesn't say it, but in order to be in his drawer, or the drawers and files of any art director, your mailer has to be able to fit in. In other words, it should be correctly sized, not more than 8½ × 11 inches.

Nothing's more annoying to an art director than a mailer that's been awkwardly sized, which he then has to fold to get into his drawer or file. What good is spending a lot of money on the production of the mailer, and then having someone spoil its artistic as well as promotional value by folding it in half? By the time they take it out for evaluation, it's been creased and battered and your beautiful photographs will end up looking like a battered accordion. That's why larger mailers are foldouts, but fall within the 8½ × 11-inch measurements.

Migliaccio also consults the directories, especially the Creative Black Book, *looking for photographers whose photographic strengths fit a job he's working on. If the job fits the photographer he's considering, he'll call in the photographer with his portfolio.*

"If it's someone I haven't seen before," he says, "I try to meet them in person. I want to see if the chemistry is right, if we can work together. That's why some art directors use the same people all the

time, because they're able to communicate on that non-verbal level of understanding.

"What I'm looking for from a photographer is someone with technical proficiency. I don't want to deal with technical problems, particularly when we get on the set. I only want to make technical adjustments after I look at the Polaroids.

"Funny thing, though. Sometimes, reps will make appointments, independent of any promotion. They'll show me a portfolio of work with a style that's perfect for a job I'm ready to shoot and the photographer gets the job. It doesn't happen often, but it does happen."

Migliaccio thinks that the type of promotions that make a difference are the ones that are utilitarian. "Calendars are good, because they stay around throughout the year. Every time you look at one, it reminds you who the photographer is.

"Posters are a good idea, especially the ones I wouldn't mind framing. Again, with a framed poster on the wall, the photographer's work is there all the time.

"The best poster I've seen was one by a photographer named Michael Pouzan. He used a big "P" in Helvetica type as a design element in the poster's layout. We eventually worked together on a job."

The biggest problem Guy Migliaccio sees with paid promotions is the rarity of follow-up. "From a marketing point of view, it would be better if they followed it up in some way. I have the same problem with reps. Sometimes they'll call and then take a while to show up wih the portfolio."

He emphasizes the necessity in targeting the audience for the promotion.

"You should narrow your marketing down to the people who'll use your type of photography. Don't shoot with a shotgun. It shows you're not thinking about your audience."

Overall, Migliaccio has a positive view of paid promotions. "I think promotions work," he says, "especially the ones that knock your feet off. You want to hire them as soon as possible.

"By and large, the quality of the photography I see is pretty good. What's impressive is the quality of work coming from the female photographers. A lot of really good work is coming from them."

DON MUNSON

Vice President and Art Director
Ballantine, Del Rey and Fawcett Books

"The promotions from photographers that really catch my eye are the ones that show they are thinking," says Don Munson. As Vice President and Art Director for Ballantine, Del Rey, and Fawcett Books, Munson's job is to oversee the production of bookcovers for mass-market paperback books. As such, he's something of a marketing specialist himself. He knows what sells, which gives him very definite ideas on what he likes to see from photographers.

"I get so many of these paid promotions in the mail (calendars, posters, and the like). It's an unrelenting volume and most of it is unoriginal. When something original comes along, it's a whole other ball of wax, which makes me sit up and take notice."

However, it is ads in directories that impress Munson even more, to the point that some of those ads have led to jobs.

"I've found photographers from their ads in American Showcase,*" he says. "Both the* Creative Black Book *and 'Showcase' are useful tools to a certain degree. The ads keep me informed of what photographers are doing. But I find that very little creativity, in general, is used in the ads in terms of design and selection of images.*

"You see a lot of good photographic clichés in the ads, things like a pencil that turns into an artist's paint brush. Stuff like that can be photographically excellent, but what really stands out is fresh imagery, *where the photographer has really thought about the content of the photographs."*

In general, Munson finds that about 10 percent of the ads in the directories are by photographers with the potential of being used. The other 90 percent produce informative ads, which might give Munson an idea or two for book covers, while he is not impressed with actual execution of the photographs.

"I like the AD Week Portfolios,*" Munson continues. "They are relatively new on the scene and I find them very exciting and a real tool. Also, in some ways, the* Creative Black Book *has become a tool as well.*

"You know, mass marketing is coming up with a concept and executing it. Ad agencies don't do that. They buy things. The concep-

tualizing is done at an earlier stage, when the client is being sold. Here, we're forever reaching and trying new things out, right up to press time. A lot of photographers find it difficult working this spontaneously."

Munson is not *cynical about photographers and their photographs. Like any client, he loves to work with photographers who can meet his needs. As for advice on what he'd like to see in promotions, Munson is very simple.*

"I already assume you're a top-notch photographer. What I want to see demonstrated visually is your ability to think and conceptualize, to produce a multi-dimensional photograph."

CHAPTER FOUR

Developing a Paid Promotion Campaign

Now that you're thinking about launching some paid promotions, you may be wondering what kind to utilize, how they should be marketed, and to whom?

Let's discuss sample promotional programs, broken down according to photographic specialty, with a special eye toward the audience for each type of promotion.

WEDDING AND PORTRAIT

Unlike the other photographic specialties that will be discussed, wedding and portrait photographers work for average people. Their audience is brides and grooms, parents who want photos of their children graduating, wives interested in boudoir photography, pet owners who want a picture of their pets, and just about anybody who, at one time or another, needs the personal services of a professional photographer.

Because they are dealing with such a wide audience, wedding and portrait photographers have to hone their marketing so that each specific promotion reaches the segment of the public desired.

Promotions should be keyed into themes, corresponding to seasons, so there's never any slack time and the photographer is always busy.

Fall

Two types of promotions should be done in the fall: sports-team photography and wedding photography.

As stated earlier, baseball and softball teams that play in the spring, begin forming in autumn. Autumn is the time to direct promotions at league officials, pitching yourself as a team photographer.

The promotion can be in the form of a brochure. Because most team photos are alike, what you're selling is not so much your photographic skill, but your skill as a businessman who can deliver, on time, what he promises. The brochure should reflect this in its copy, which will outline your services and how much they cost. Also included will be the name of the studio, your name, address, and phone number, though you'll be doing follow-up calls anyway. You should also have a few of your best team photos in the layout, to demonstrate your skill as a photographer.

Why a brochure rather than a flyer? A well-designed brochure will make you look like a successful professional, which is the image you want to project. It tells the person who's thinking about hiring you that you're prosperous. If you list some of your former clients in the brochure, you'll also be saying that you're reliable.

The second type of promotion to do in the fall is weddings. Though weddings occur all year 'round, summer is the common season for them, so fall is an ideal time to start pitching the wedding business.

Consider saturating your town with flyers extolling your virtues as a wedding photographer. Remember that print quality is not all that great, so use only one photograph that reproduces well, on the flyer.

The flyer should contain information about your services, but do not discuss price. You're not appealing to someone like the president of a little league, who can let a contract for the whole league and wants to know cost up front. You're appealing to average people who aren't aware of pricing, and might be initially turned off by figures. Once you get them in the studio, then you can discuss cost.

Flyers can also be sent by direct mail to former clients and referrals. You can also check the engagement notices in your local paper and add the names of those recently engaged to your mailing list.

If you have the money, you might want to consider sending

brochures rather than flyers by direct mail. Unlike the brochures to teams, brochures to prospective brides and grooms might have a larger assortment of high-quality wedding photographs, proving you're an expert in your field.

Winter

Winter is a good time to push your services as a portrait photographer to both captains of business and the families of graduating seniors.

Use a brochure, containing executive portraits you've taken and some brief copy outlining your services, as a promotional tool, directed by mail toward the company executives in your area. You can compile your mailing list through personal knowledge, referrals, and by thumbing through the *Yellow Pages*, making note of the companies you want to solicit, and then simply calling the general switchboard to get the names of the people you need to contact.

Parents of graduating seniors can be contacted by placing an ad in local papers. This is an effective means of contacting a lot of people very quickly. You might also want to consider advertising in school publications as well, such as student newspapers and magazines.

Spring

So far, we've been discussing promoting the bread-and-butter of the wedding and portrait photographer's trade. But what happens if this is not the only type of photography you want to do?

The spring is a good time to begin marketing yourself in other photographic areas you wish to enter. For instance, if you want to be a commercial photographer, put together a self-assigned portfolio of commercial shots, get a graphic designer to help you design an ad, and then take a page out in one of the photography directories.

Don't go with a national directory; the competition is too heavy. Pick a regional directory that's affordable and will give you reprints to be used in a direct-mail promotion to potential commercial clients in your area.

Summer

What do people do in the summer? They take their clothes off. They want to go to the beach, the pool, or the cabana club and soak away that summer heat and show off those bodies they've been perfecting all winter in their health clubs. That's why summer is a good time to promote boudoir photography.

Like Rudy Pollak, buy some ads in local newspapers, promoting your services as a boudoir photographer. You may be surprised at the responses you get.

COMMERCIAL PHOTOGRAPHERS

The first thing a commercial photographer should consider is hiring a good graphic designer like Kimberly Prezyna, or a firm like PM Associates.

Unless you have a background in graphic design, it's just too difficult to attempt a successful promotional program by doing it yourself. Spend the money and hire the expert.

Get a package price from the designer for at least three different promotional elements. Let's say they are mailers, directory-page ads, and posters.

Directory-page ads are the simplest. Have the expert help you pick the images. Then target the directory which gives you the most value for your money. That is, which directory reaches the audience you want to hit for the least amount of money? Regional or national? These are questions you'll have to answer for yourself, but you can expedite the decision by looking at the directories' mailing lists and seeing if the people and agencies you want to reach are on it.

As stated earlier, knowing who you want to reach is all-important, and the people commercial photographers want to contact are art directors and art buyers at advertising agencies. They are the ones who work with photographers to produce the ads you want to shoot.

So, a snazzily designed mailer should be sent to the art directors and art buyers at the agencies you're interested in.

Art buyers essentially screen the photographer's promotions and make decisions about which ones to direct to the attention of the art directors. The art directors make the final decision on who to hire to shoot the job, on the basis of their own opinion and the recommendation of the art buyer. Once that decision is made, the art buyer works with the photographer laying out the financial terms of the business arrangement.

In addition to art directors and art buyers, you might want to send your mailer to any production people you know personally at the agency. While production people are much further down the totem pole—they work on the actual production of the ad once the photographs have been shot—they may be in a position to have the "ear" of an art buyer or art director. If this is the case, you should make sure they receive your promotion as well.

One other person you may come in contact with at the agency is the creative director, who is above the art director. The creative director is essentially the quarterback, in charge of not only the look of the ad but the copy as well. They rarely get involved in the photographer-selection process. For that reason, sending them promotional materials is a waste of time and money, unless you already have a relationship.

Narrow the promotion even further. Consider what kind of clients you want to work with. Do you want to shoot beverages, beauty products, food, or something else? Whatever it is, there's an advertising agency that represents just about every product or service you can think of, from Jean Naté perfume to McDonald's. At each agency, there are one or more art directors who work on those particular accounts. How do you find out which agencies represent which clients and who the art directors are for those accounts?

You'll find a reference book at the library that will prove to be invaluable in answering these questions. It's called *The Standard Directory of Advertising Agencies*. It's published quarterly. Also known as "The Agency Red Book," it lists agencies geographically and then alphabetically. The latter listings include names, addresses, phone numbers, listings of accounts, annual billings, and agency personnel, including art directors.

For more information, you can write the publication directly at 3004 Glenview Road, Wilmette, IL 60091, or call (312) 256-6067.

Specific marketing becomes very important when you're sending out the more expensive promotional items like posters, catalogues, brochures, and calendars. It's too expensive to saturate every agency. But by narrowing it down to the art directors and art buyers who work on the accounts you're interested in shooting for, you have a better chance of getting their interest with your photography, which should be oriented toward the art directors' and art buyers' areas of specialization.

FASHION PHOTOGRAPHERS

Fashion photographers exist in a glamorous world and their paid promotions should reflect this fact accordingly. As with commercial photographers, the paid promotions of a fashion photographer should be directed at art directors and art buyers. They should also be directed at the editors of the fashion magazines, who regularly hire fashion photographers to shoot editorial layouts.

Because fashions change so frequently, the photographs you use in your promotions should not only reflect your skills as a photographer, they should also show fashions currently in style. You don't want to appear behind the times.

What kinds of promotions are we talking about? You're definitely going to have to have a mailer, which will not only be sent out, but also left off as a reminder of who you are after you show your portfolio.

Some sort of brochure, especially the fold-out type, would be another good way to show your photography to a client. Again, you're going to want some expert help in designing any of the paid promotions being discussed.

Art directors seem especially to like posters and calendars. Calendars are synonymous with beautiful women, who are the stock and trade of fashion photography, so it shouldn't be a problem finding the images to make a calendar. As for posters, what better way to promote your photography than selecting a couple of your hottest images, getting a graphic designer to do a great layout for you, printing them up in poster form, and then sending them to art directors and art buyers?

I've left catalogs for last, because shooting a catalog really amounts to going out and getting the assignment to do just that. It's not really a form of paid promotion until you actually have it printed up to send to potential clients, which can cost a lot of money.

Still, if you contact the different stores in your area that sell clothing, or such luxury items as jewelry, antiques, expensive cars and rare coins, you may be able to convince them to let you shoot their catalog for a fee. The catalog could then become a paid promotion as previously outlined.

Now we get to the directory page. Because fashion photographers exist in such a competitive marketplace, you may want to advertise in more than one directory, considering a combination of national and regional publications as your budget permits.

Remember that once the promotion goes out, it should be tracked and you should be making your follow-up calls. I can't emphasize this enough.

CORPORATE PHOTOGRAPHY

Corporate photographers are hired by designers of annual reports and brochures that major companies print up for their stockholders. These designers are the audience for the corporate photographer's paid promotion.

If you're going to buy a directory page, buy it in *American Corporate Showcase*. The market has already been selected for you. All you have to do is supply the page.

Corporate photographers have the same choice of paid promotional elements that other photographers do, but it's easier to narrow down the choices because of the subjects involved.

Corporate photographers frequently shoot in factories. While the skilled photographer can make even the most menial and boring tasks look exciting through the use of dynamic visual graphics and mastery of lighting, by and large, corporate photography is not the stuff that great posters or calendars are made of.

Corporate photographers should instead concentrate their promotional efforts on eye-catching mailers and brochures. Include the full range of your work, particularly if you've taken some good executive portraiture. Sent to the designers of corporate publications and annual reports (get a copy of *American Corporate Showcase*'s mailing list), these pieces should feature the photographs that best illustrate your abilities.

When you've been involved in an annual report or other corporate publication that you're particularly proud of, don't forget to request extra copies. If your supply is limited, you can still use these as special mailers to clients with whom you particularly want to work.

PHOTOJOURNALISTS

Photojournalists are going to be marketing their skills to the people who regularly employ them: the editors of newspapers and magazines. Keep in mind, these individuals tend to be rather cynical and not easily bowled over.

One way to impress them is with a poster depicting some of the famous people you've photographed, much like William Coupon did. Or the poster might have a couple of terrific shots that are memorable.

A second way to impress editors would be with something practical, like a calendar. Each month would be represented by one of your photos, perhaps corresponding to the season.

By using *Writer's Market*, a sourcebook published by Writer's Digest Books, or by going through current issues of *Editor and Publisher* and other reference books at your local library, you can compile a list of editors who hire photographers to shoot jobs for their publication.

If you haven't already expanded into photographing people for advertising, you may want to consider buying a directory page. Frequently, art directors need the skills photojournalists have of working with people to shoot people-type ads. While it may not pay to launch a full-scale paid promotion directed at art directors and art buyers, it may pay to put together a directory page with some of your best people shots.

A Valuable Source

Photographers who are getting together mailing lists of art directors, art buyers, and other creative personnel who might have use of a photographer's talents, can turn to Creative Access as a valuable source of information.

Creative Access is a service agency that sells photographers lists of personnel who hire photographers. The lists are broken down by photographic specialty and geography, then subdivided into art directors, creative directors, designers, and so on.

The lists come in a number of formats. There are lists on peel and stick labels, which are ready to mail. There are cheshire lists, that go to mailing houses who do the mailings for you. There are lists on long sheets of paper, called galleys, so you can select the ones you're especially interested in and want to address your promotion to. If you have a computer, the lists also come on floppy discs.

All lists are constantly updated and because of that, are designed for one-time use. If you want to get more information about Creative Access, here's their address and phone number: Creative Access, 415 N. Superior, Chicago, IL 60610, telephone 1 (800) 422-3771.

Tracking Your Promotions. Regardless of the type of promotion you undertake, you will have wasted your money unless you track it. Keep a written record in a notebook of who gets what and follow up the promotion with a letter and phone call two weeks after the promotion goes out. Make sure the promotion has been received by the interested party. If not, get another one out immediately.

During the follow-up call, when you get the art director or art buyer on the phone (it's not all that difficult if you keep calling), ask them if they've seen the promotion. If they have, don't ask if they liked it. They probably won't tell you the truth anyway. What is important is that you've made contact. Ask for an appointment to show your portfolio. Then go in and knock 'em dead.

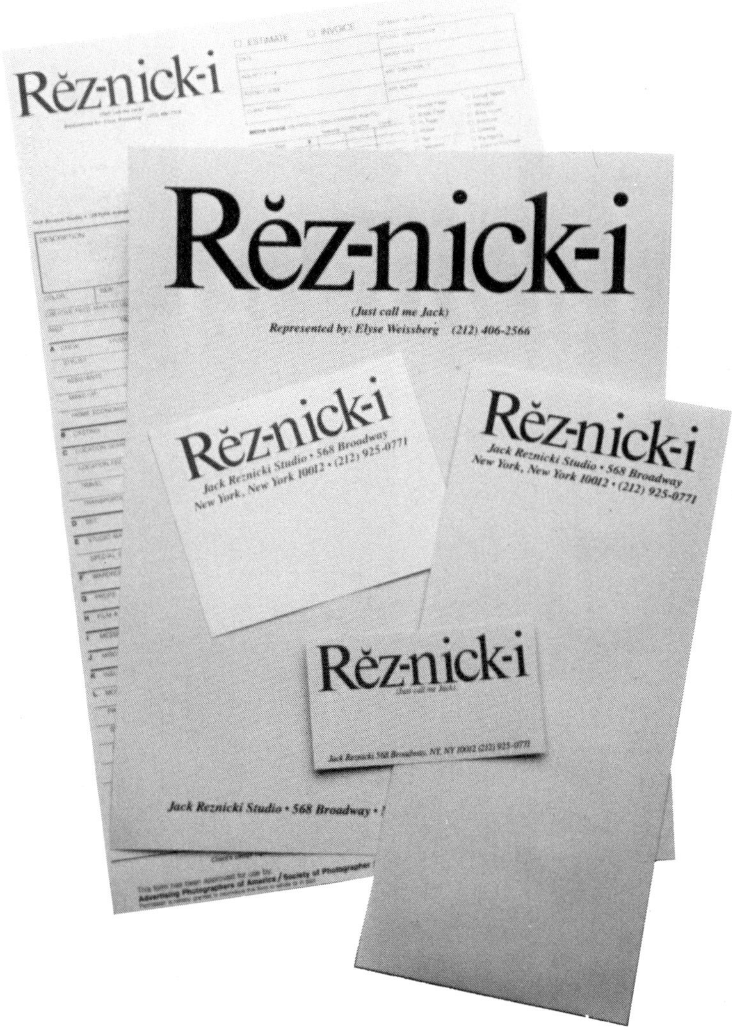

New York-based photographer Jack Reznicki has developed a distinctive logo, which is prominently featured on all of his promotional efforts. A humorous take-off on his often-mispronounced last name, Reznicki is spelled out phonetically in bold letters, while the retort "Just call me Jack" appears below.

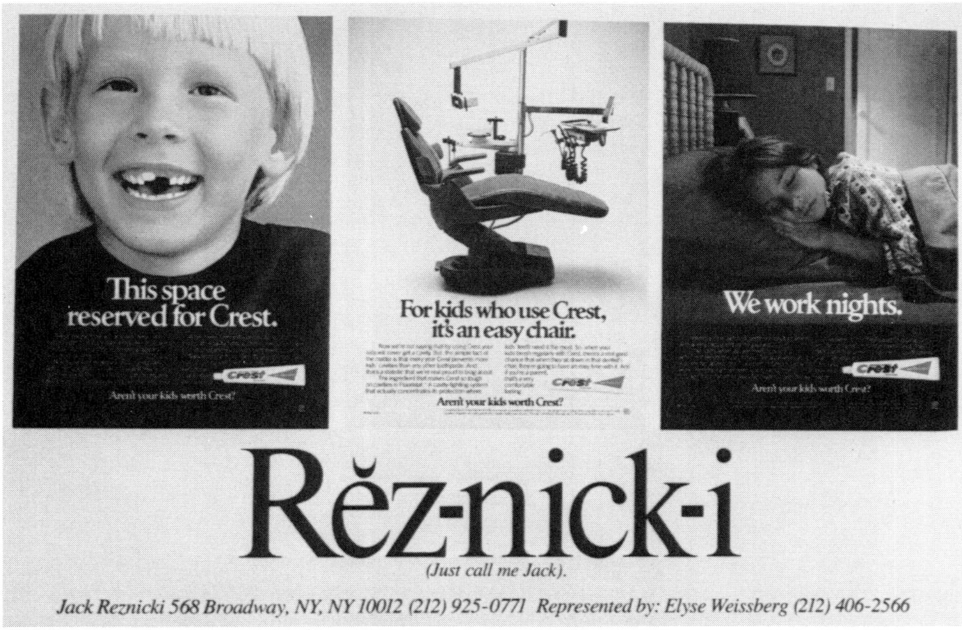

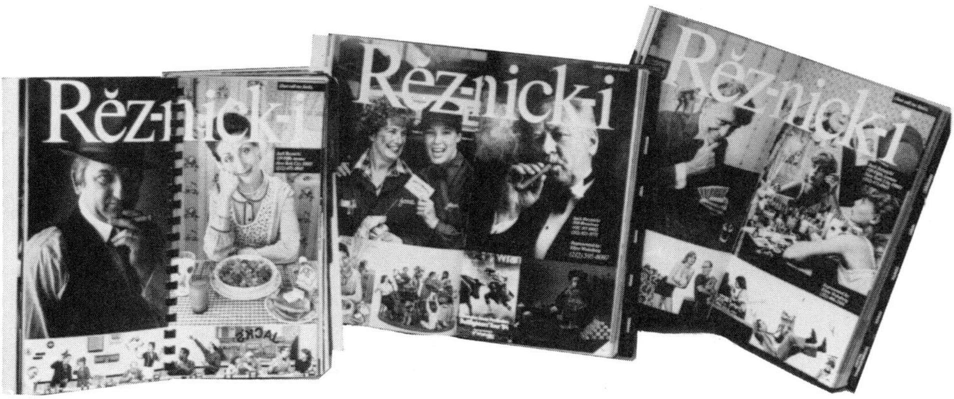

Here are some examples of Reznicki's paid promotional efforts, including double-page spreads in the *Creative Black Book* and printed mailers. Each exhibits his strength in working with people in illustrative situations, but notice how his name receives equal emphasis—this maintains a strong association between his photography and his name in the client's mind.

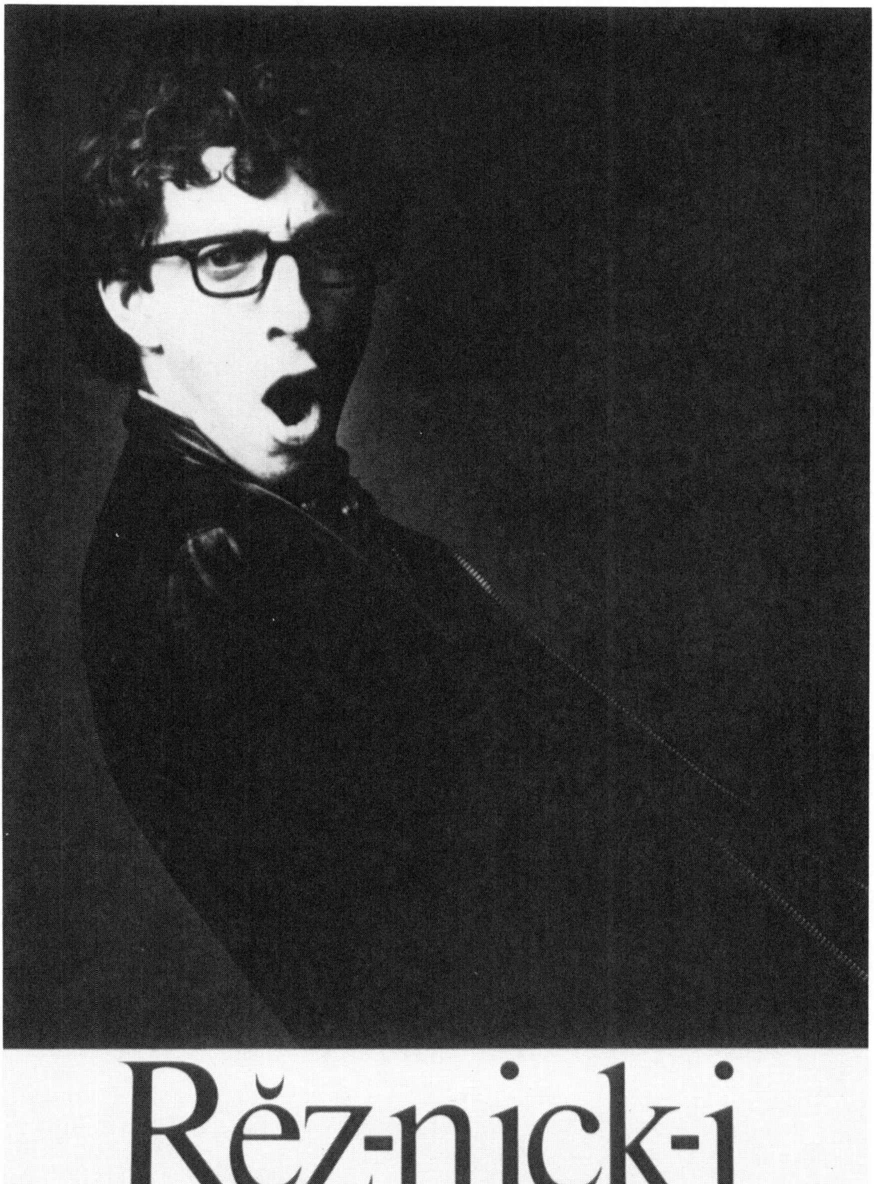
Rěz-nick-i
(Just call me Jack).
Jack Reznicki 568 Broadway, NY, NY 10012 (212) 925-0771
Represented by: Elyse Weissberg (212) 406-2566

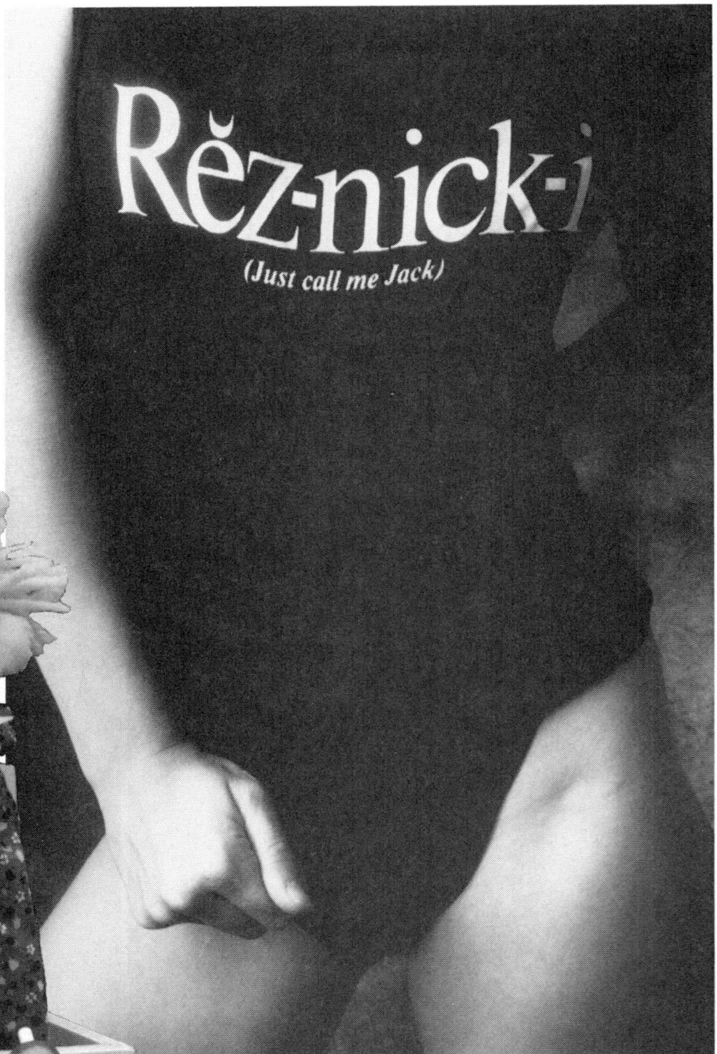

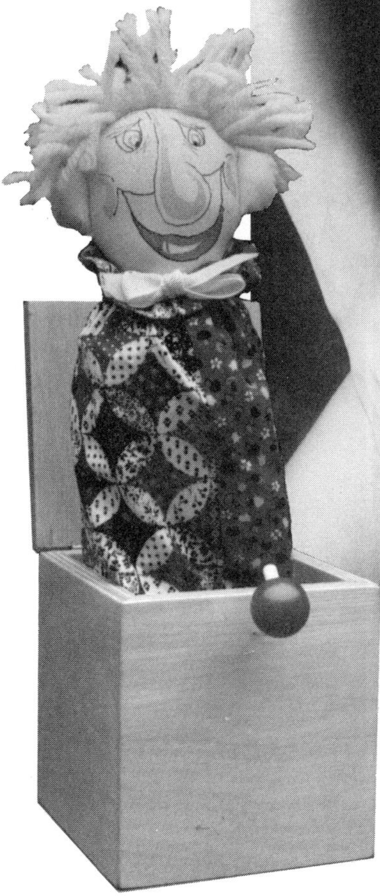

Reznicki's clever specialized promotions are well-remembered by recipients. Shown here are some of his recent holiday gifts to clients and potential clients: a t-shirt featuring his logo, a jack-in-a-box toy, a tin of home-baked cookies, and a small jug of "private label" apple cider.

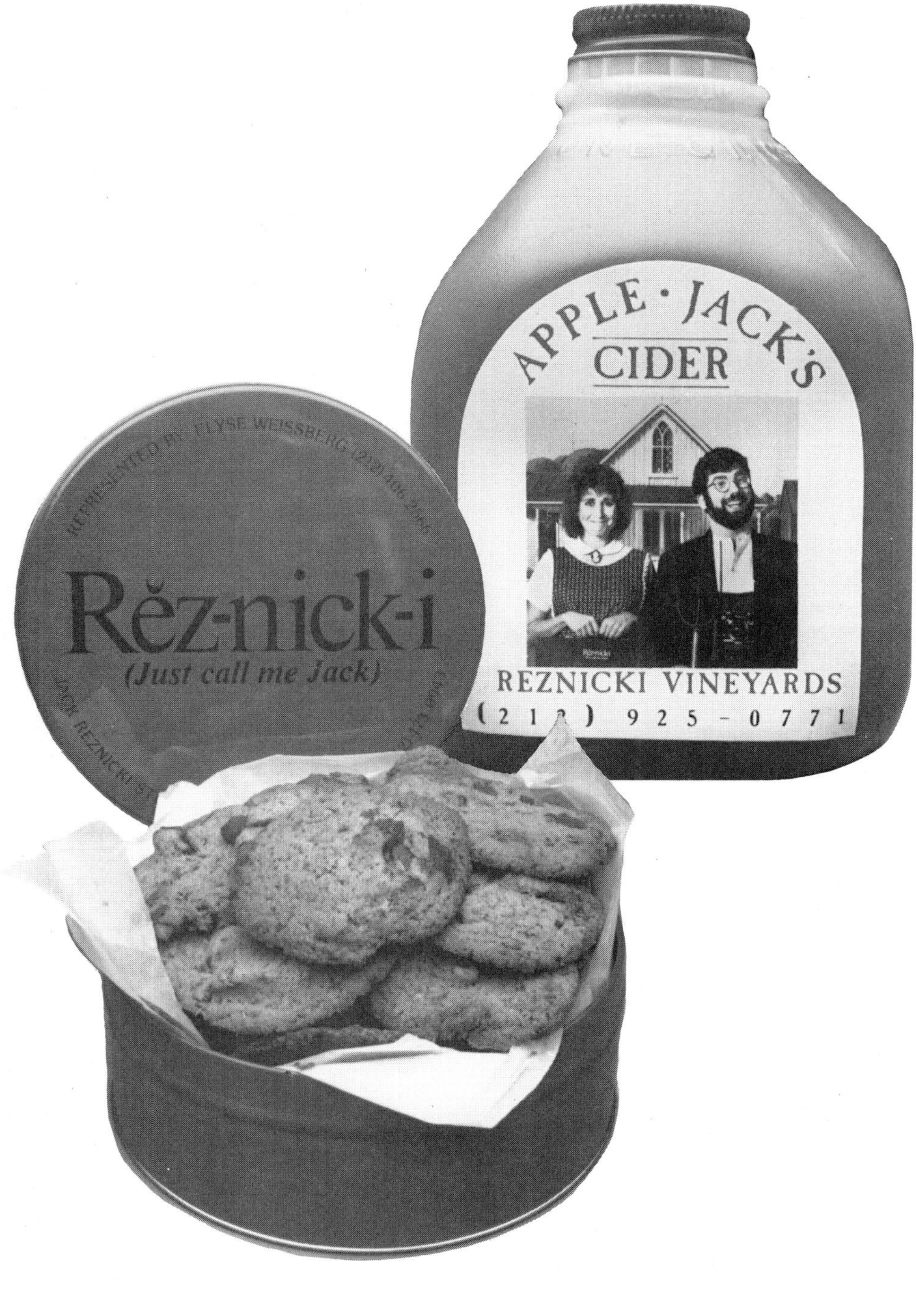
APPLE • JACK'S
CIDER
REZNICKI VINEYARDS
Rĕz-nick-i
(Just call me Jack)
REPRESENTED BY ELYSE WEISSBERG (212) 406-2566

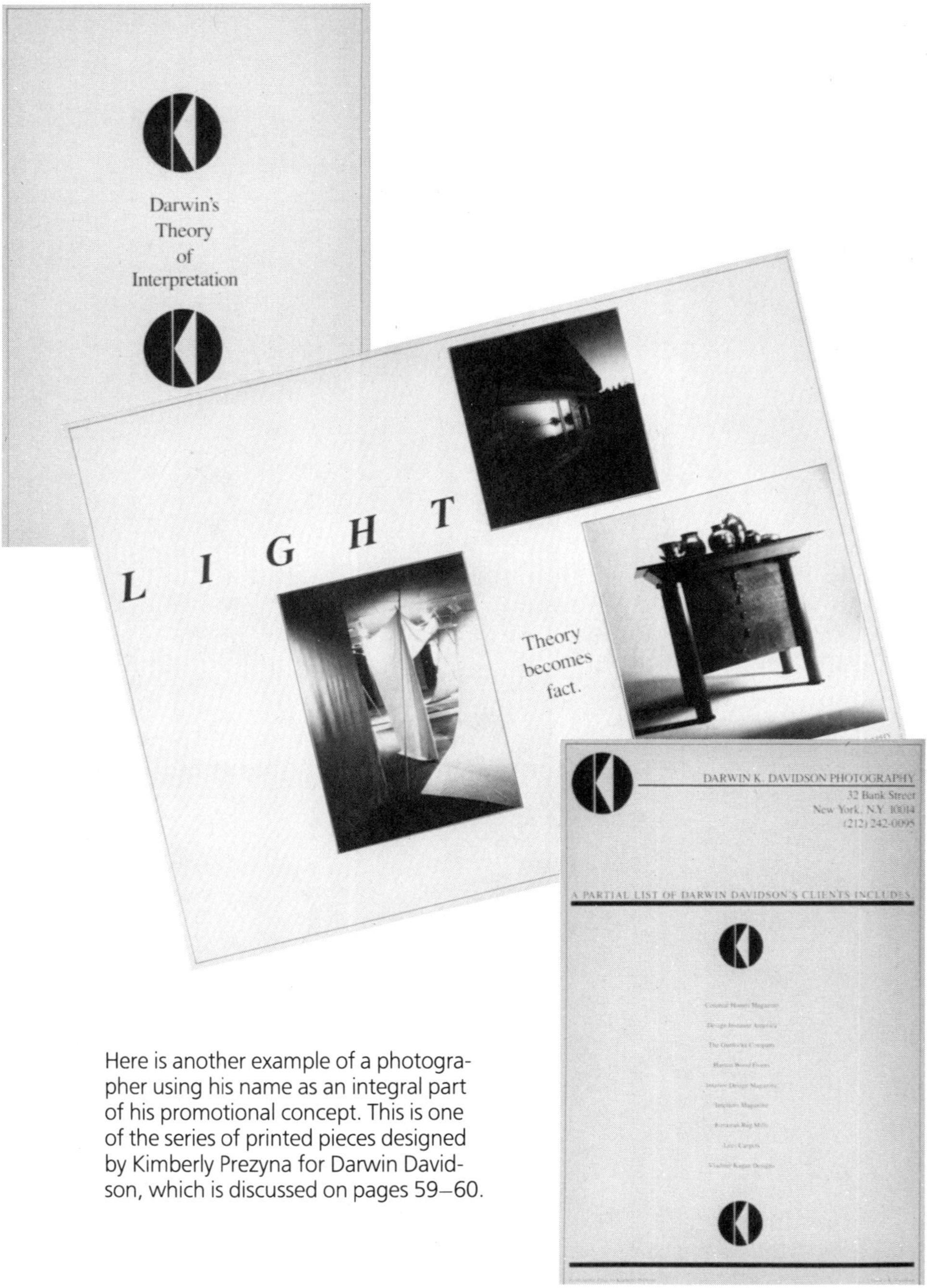

Here is another example of a photographer using his name as an integral part of his promotional concept. This is one of the series of printed pieces designed by Kimberly Prezyna for Darwin Davidson, which is discussed on pages 59–60.

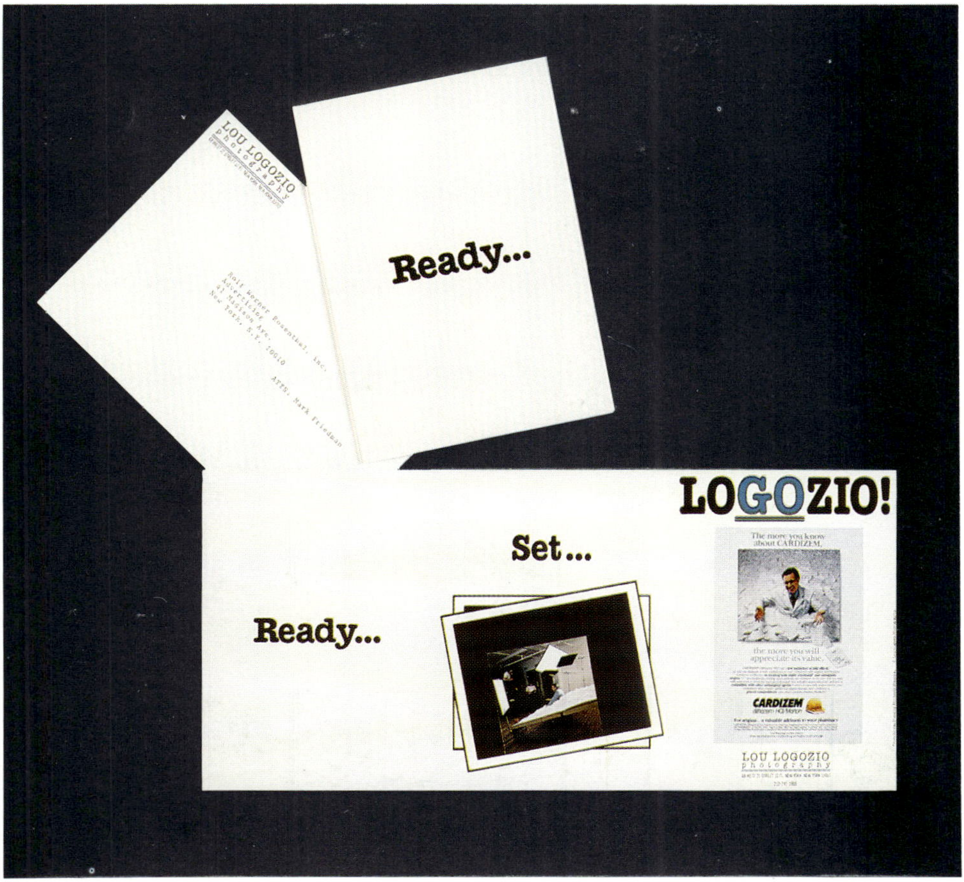

Here is another example of how designer Kimberly Prezyna has developed a promotional piece around a concept featuring the photographer's name, this time for Lou Logozio. Prezyna obviously understands the promotional value in establishing an identity for the photographer as well as for his or her work.

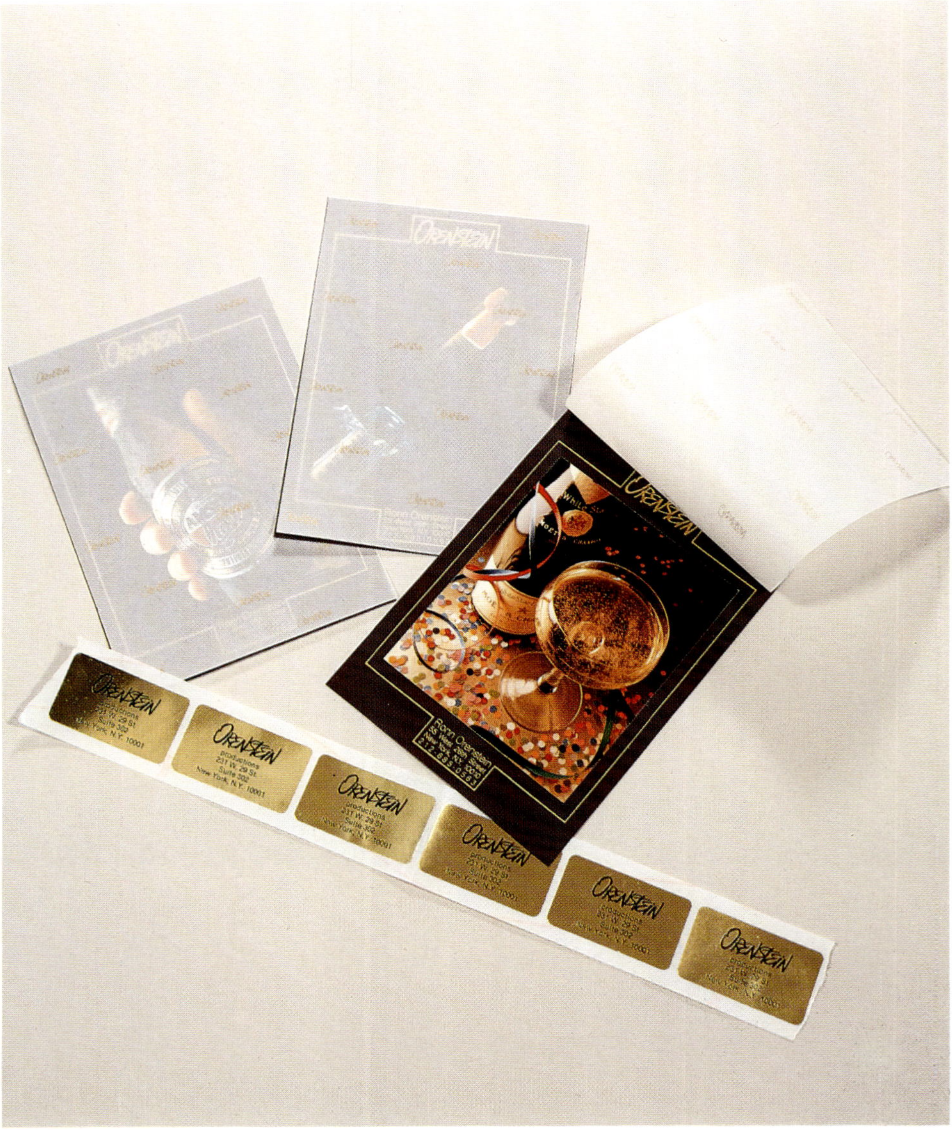
Ronn Orenstein
55 West 26th Street
New York, N.Y. 10010
212-685-0563
Orenstein
productions
231 W. 29 St.
Suite 302
New York, N.Y. 10001

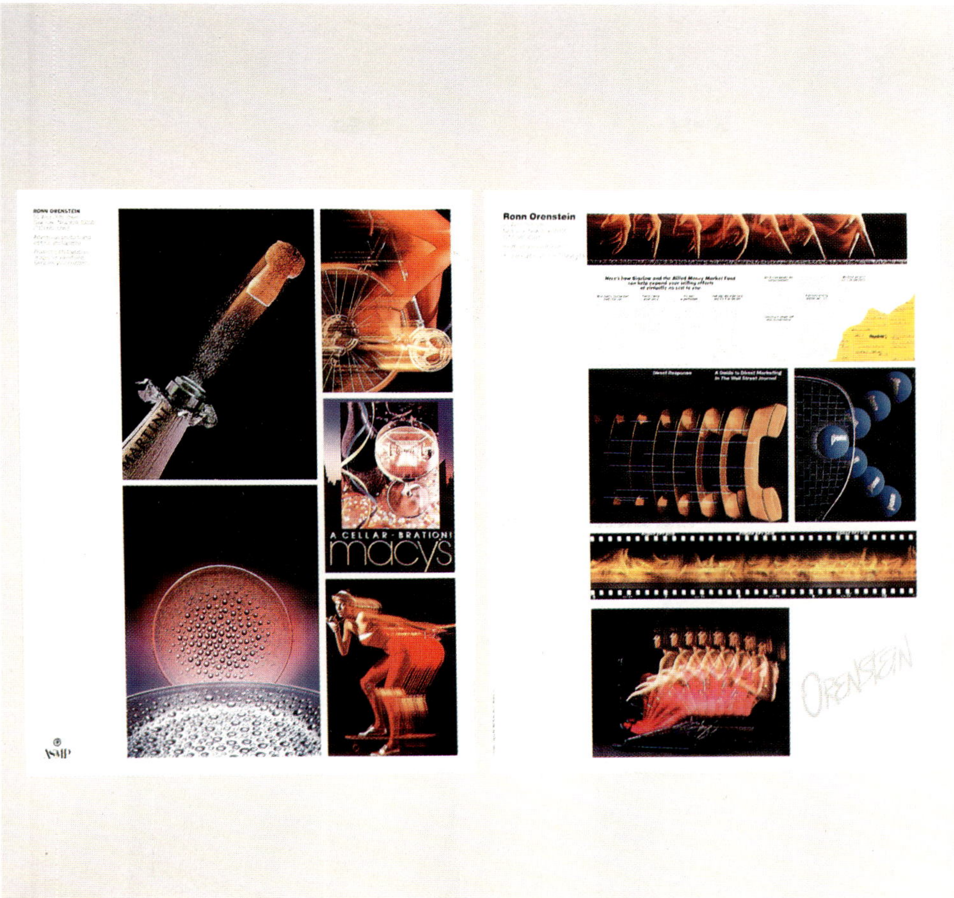

The intriguing mailer that Kimberly Prezyna designed for Ronn Orenstein is shown on the opposite page. Simple, yet elegant, I find this promotion to be much more representative of the quality of Orenstein's work than his advertisements in *American Showcase*, which are shown above. The layout of these pages is terribly busy, and tend to draw attention away from the photographs.

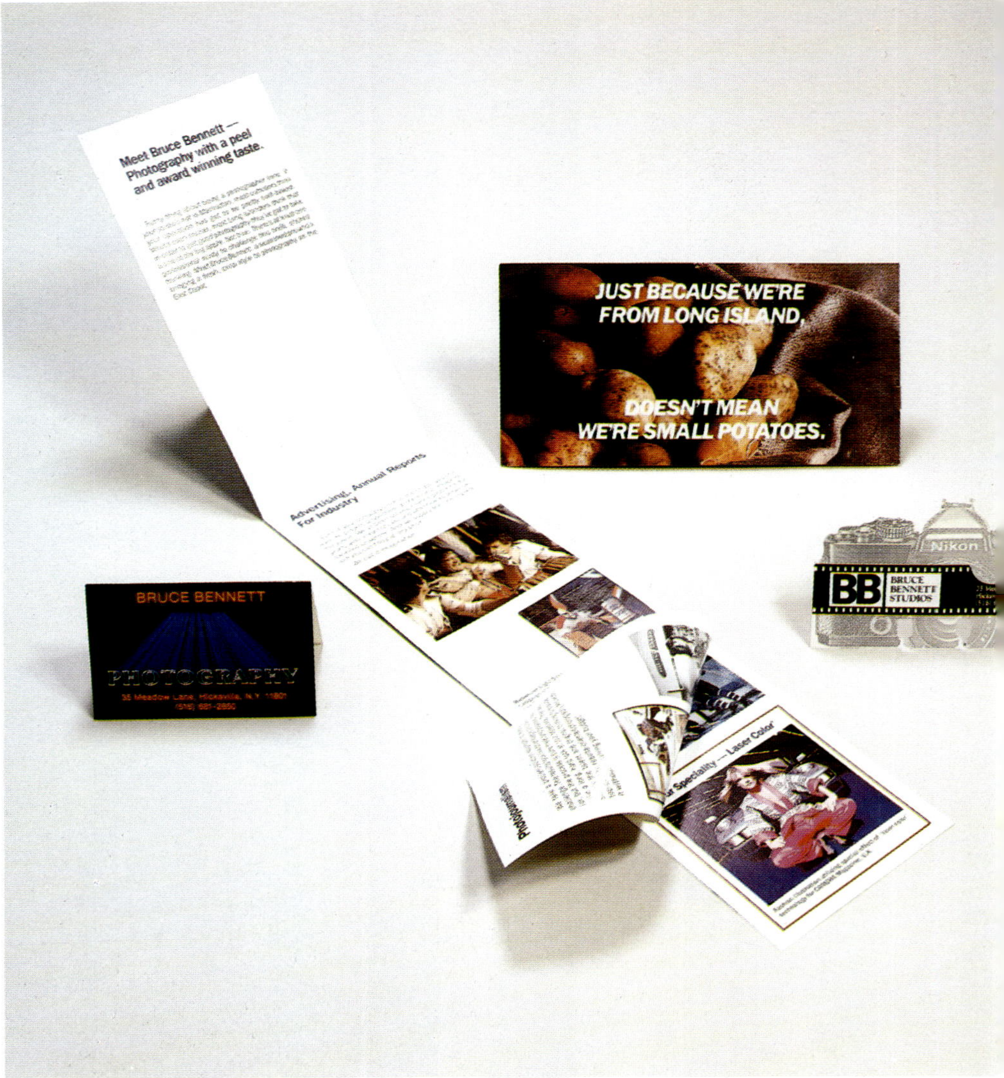
Meet Bruce Bennett —
Photography with a peel
and award winning taste.
JUST BECAUSE WE'RE
FROM LONG ISLAND,
DOESN'T MEAN
WE'RE SMALL POTATOES.
Advertising, Annual Reports
For Industry
BRUCE BENNETT
PHOTOGRAPHY
Nikon
BB
BRUCE
BENNETT
STUDIOS

Long Island-based photographer Bruce Bennett's promotional material includes a brochure and a business card, both of which are sent to prospective clients. Also shown is his "potato" promotion (which is discussed on page 57), and a mailer featuring Bennett's logo and address superimposed on a Nikon camera.

One of Bennett's more original promotions is shown below: a t-shirt with silk-screened bullet holes and the copy "I got shot . . . at Bruce Bennett Studios" running underneath.

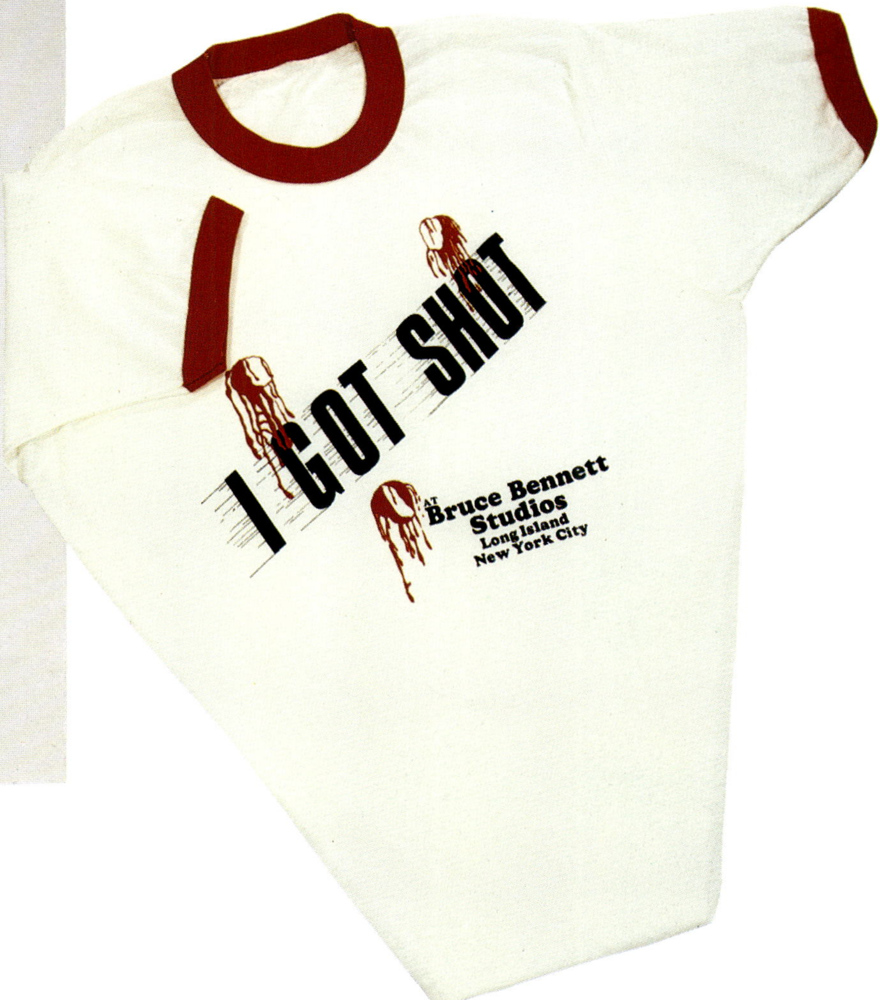

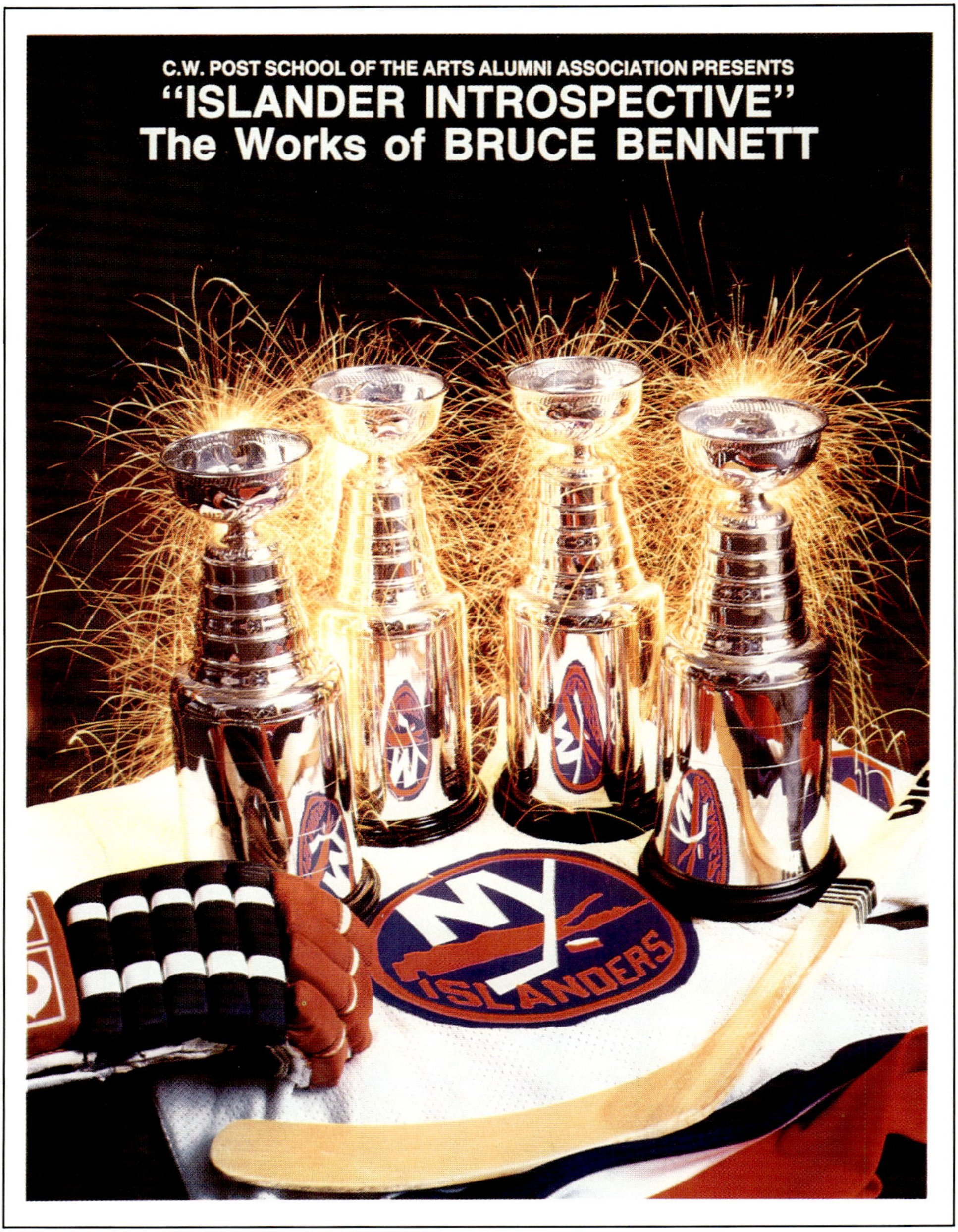
C.W. POST SCHOOL OF THE ARTS ALUMNI ASSOCIATION PRESENTS
"ISLANDER INTROSPECTIVE"
The Works of BRUCE BENNETT
NY
ISLANDERS

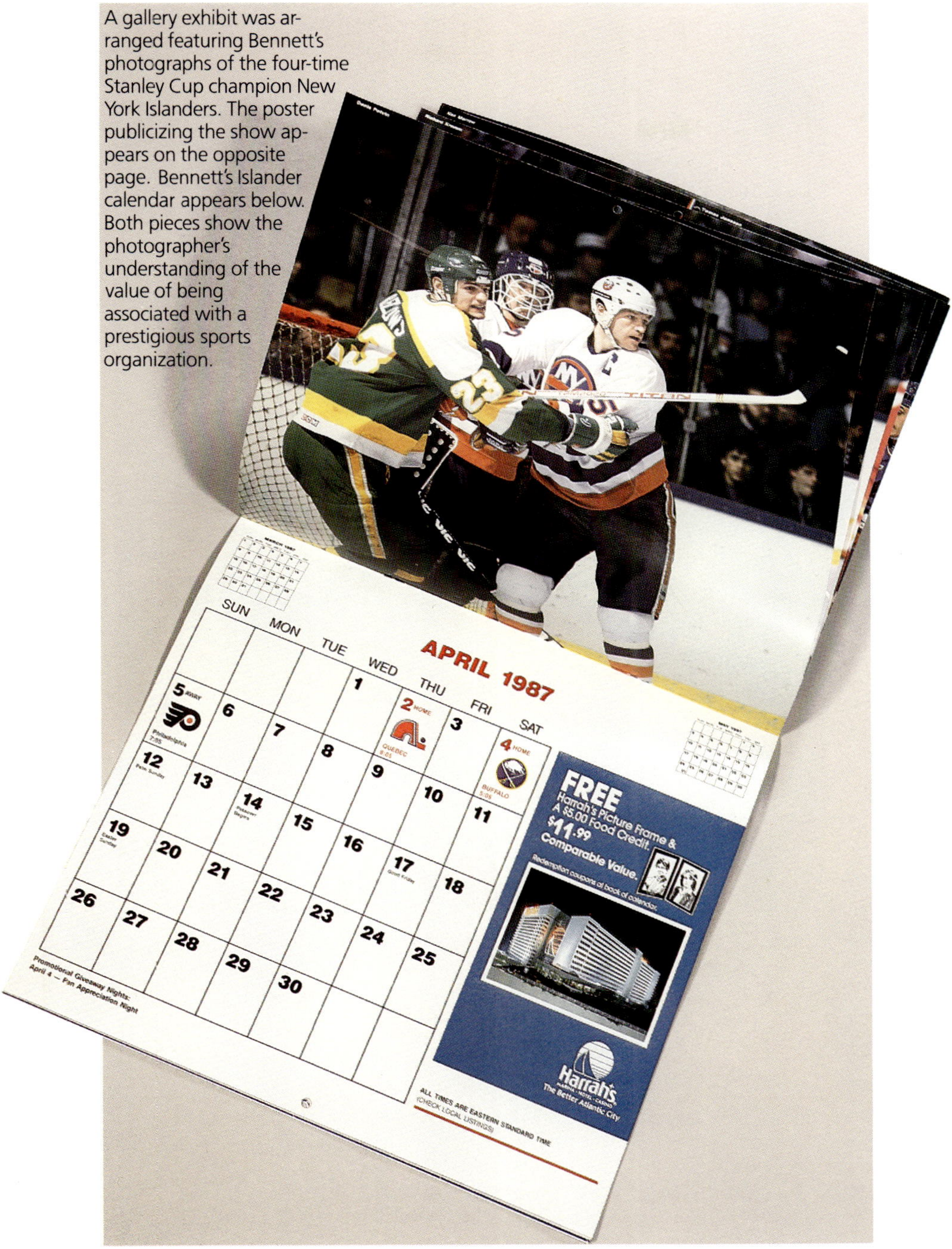

A gallery exhibit was arranged featuring Bennett's photographs of the four-time Stanley Cup champion New York Islanders. The poster publicizing the show appears on the opposite page. Bennett's Islander calendar appears below. Both pieces show the photographer's understanding of the value of being associated with a prestigious sports organization.

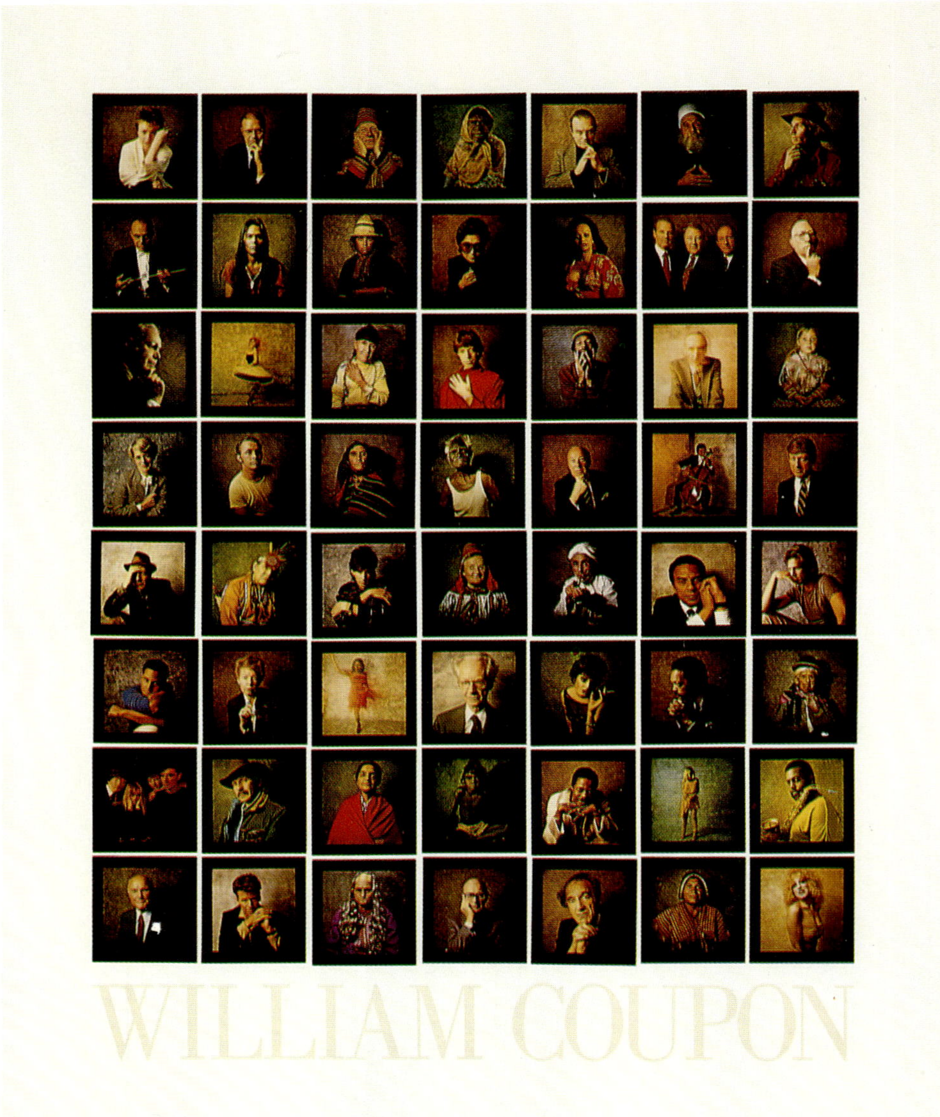

William Coupon has concentrated his promotional efforts in the area of posters. His first is a strikingly designed combination of famous personalities and others, mixed together to show his talent for working with a wide range of people. The second singles out the Talking Heads' David Byrne. A third poster features people in a variety of settings.

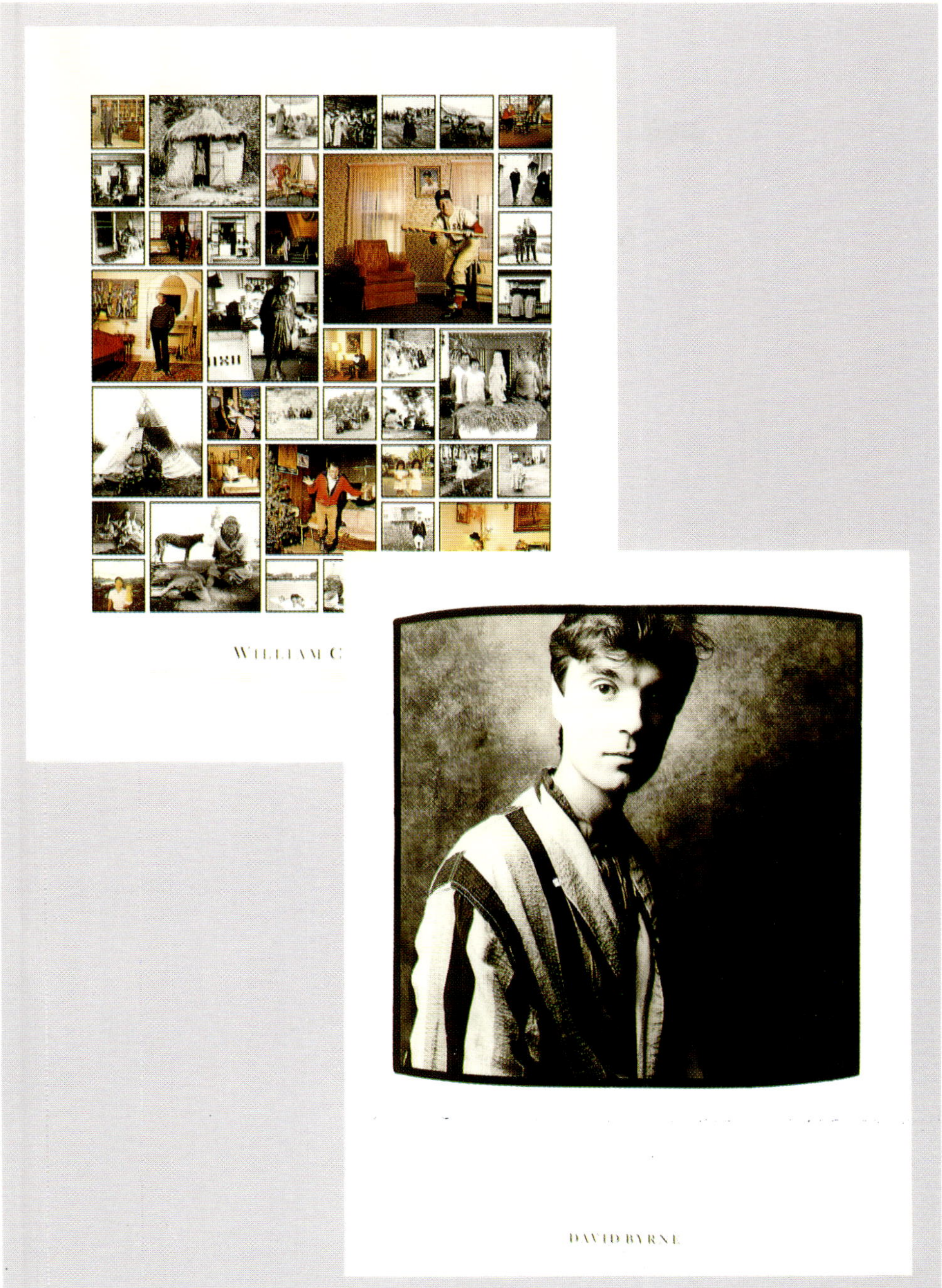
WILLIAM
DAVID BYRNE

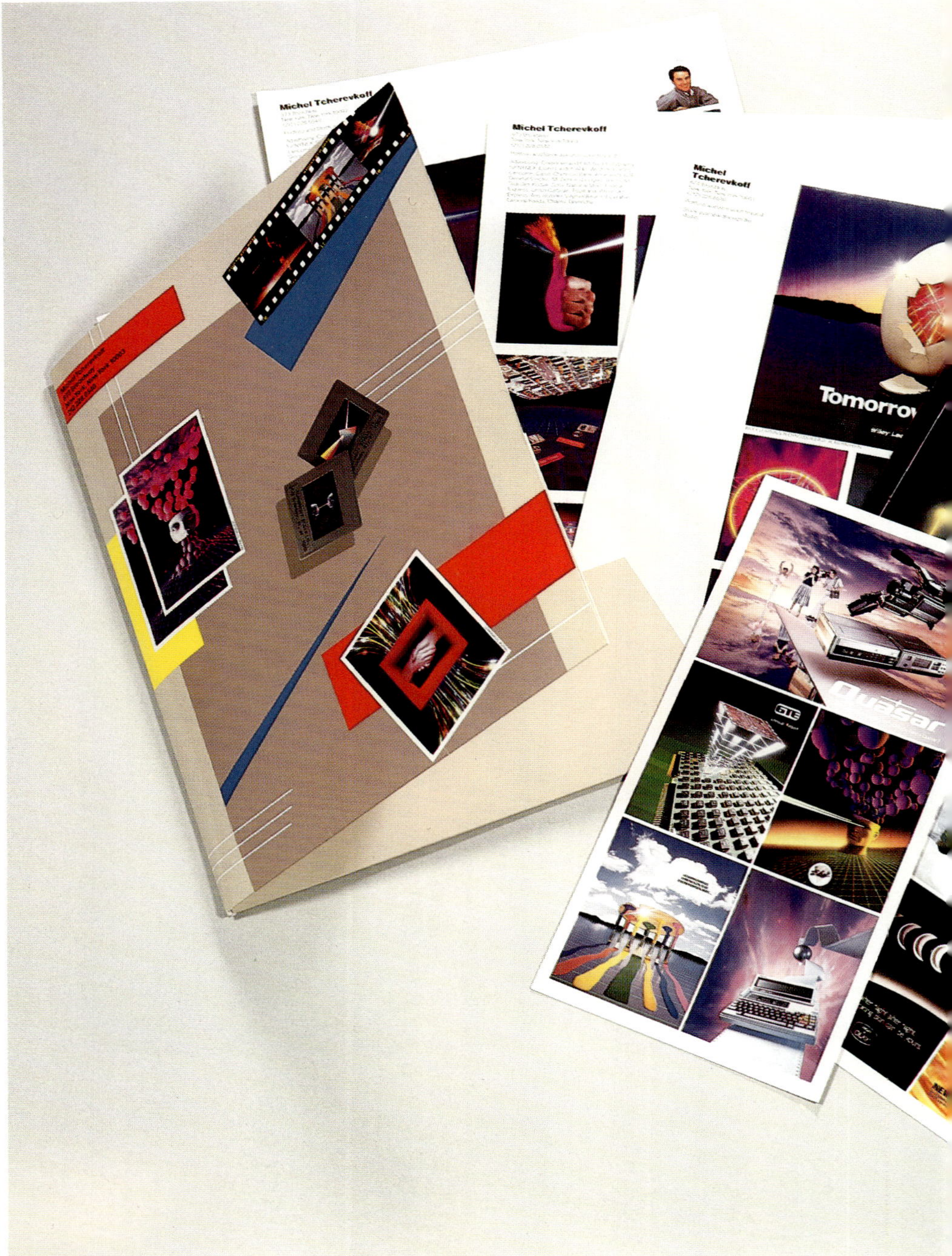
Michel Tcherevkoff
Michel Tcherevkoff
Michel
Tcherevkoff
Tomorrow
Quasar

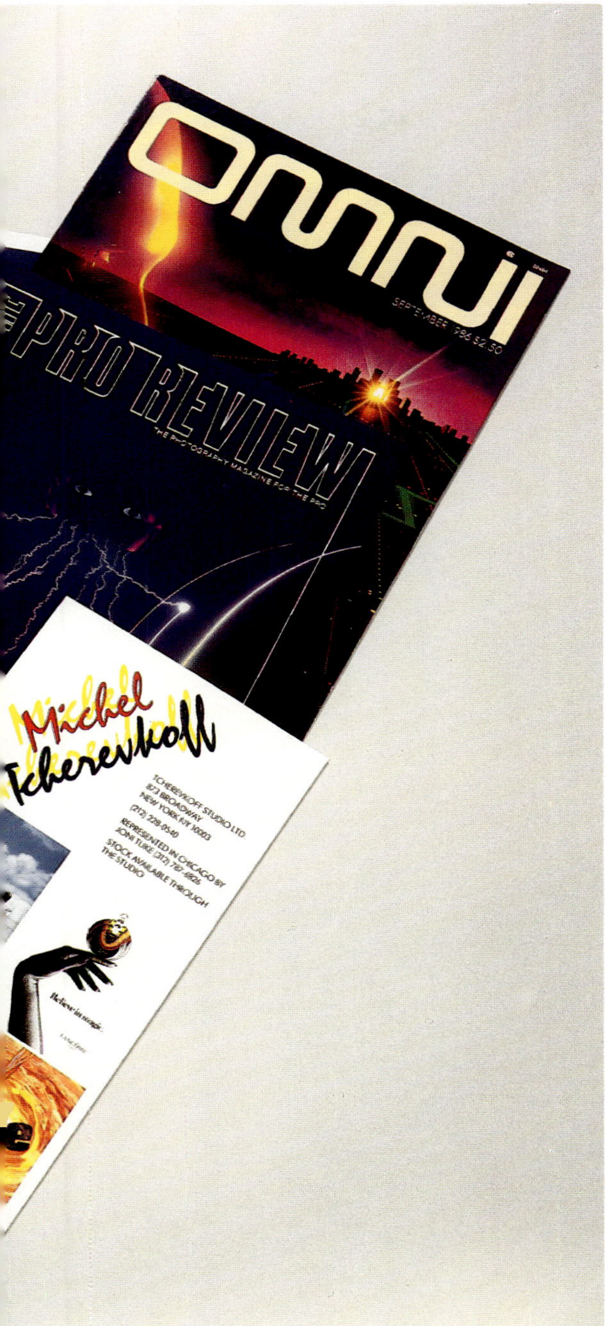

Special-effects photographer Michel Tcherevkoff truly understands the value of self-promotion. Shown here is his publicity kit, which is a folder containing many different elements.

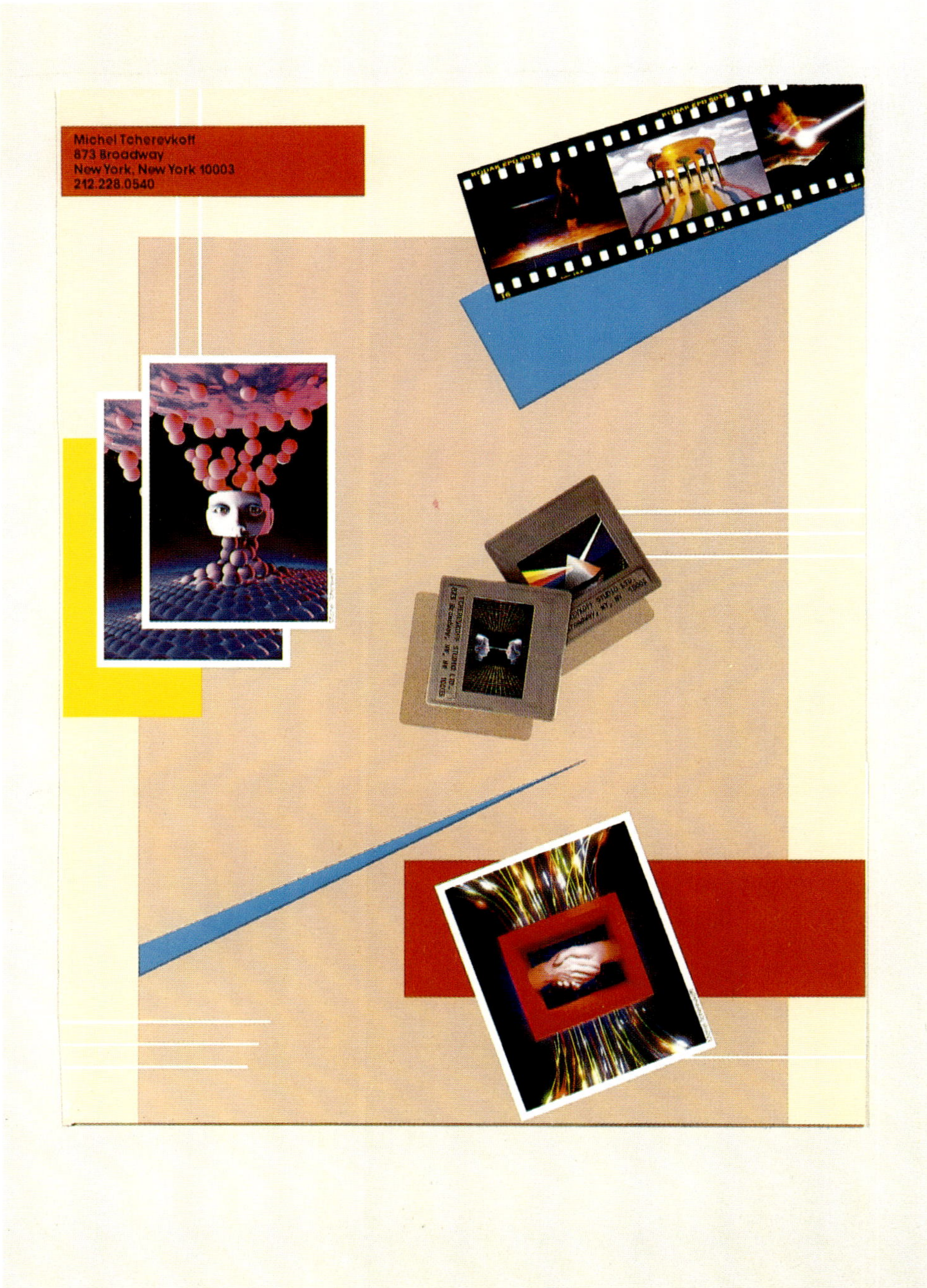
Michel Tcherevkoff
873 Broadway
New York, New York 10003
212.228.0540

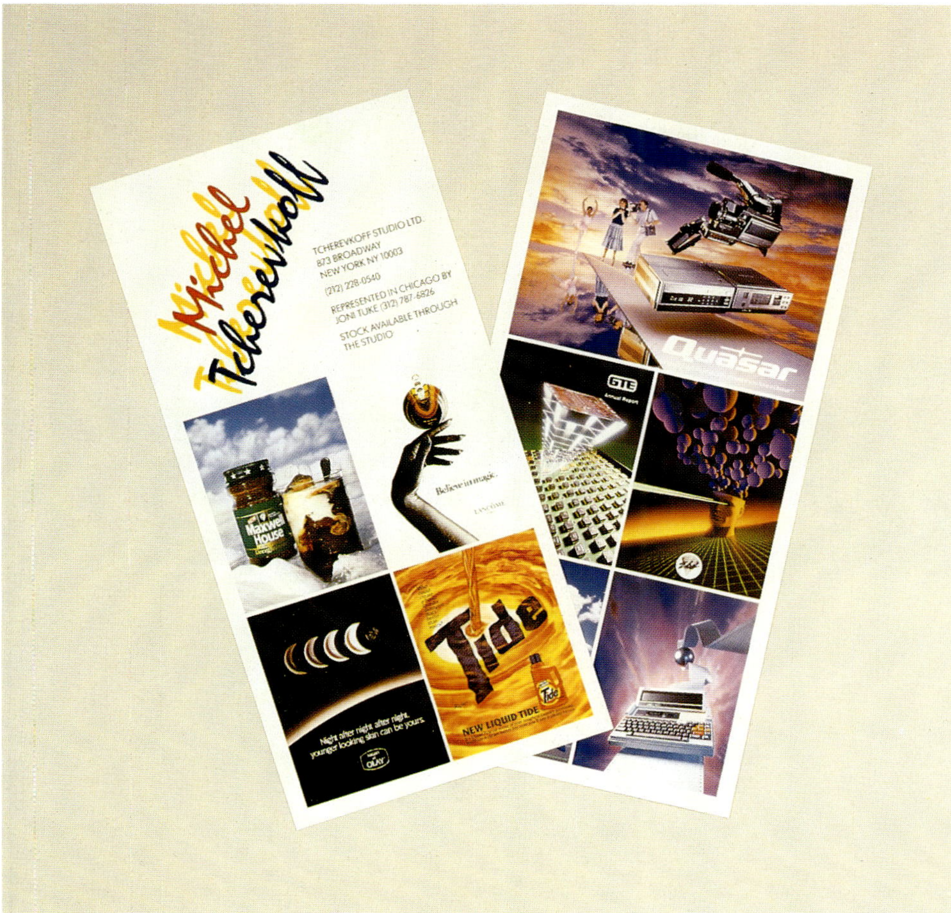

Tcherevkoff's folder (opposite) is cleverly designed and well printed. Some of his most famous photographs, as well as his name and address, appear on the front and back covers. Tcherevkoff also uses direct mail pieces (above) as a separate promotion, but they're included in the kit as well.

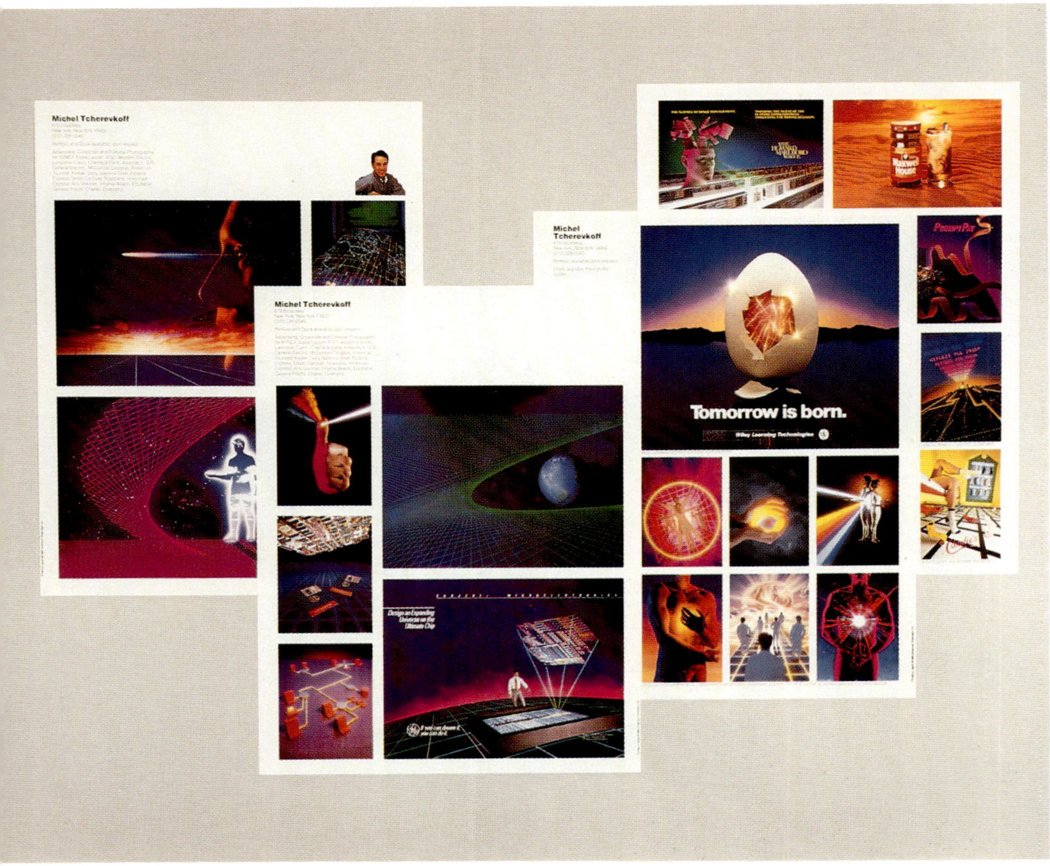

Reprints of directory-page advertisements are offered to photographers. Shown here are some of Tcherevkoff's most recent pages in *American Showcase*. Of course, they also go in the promotion kit.

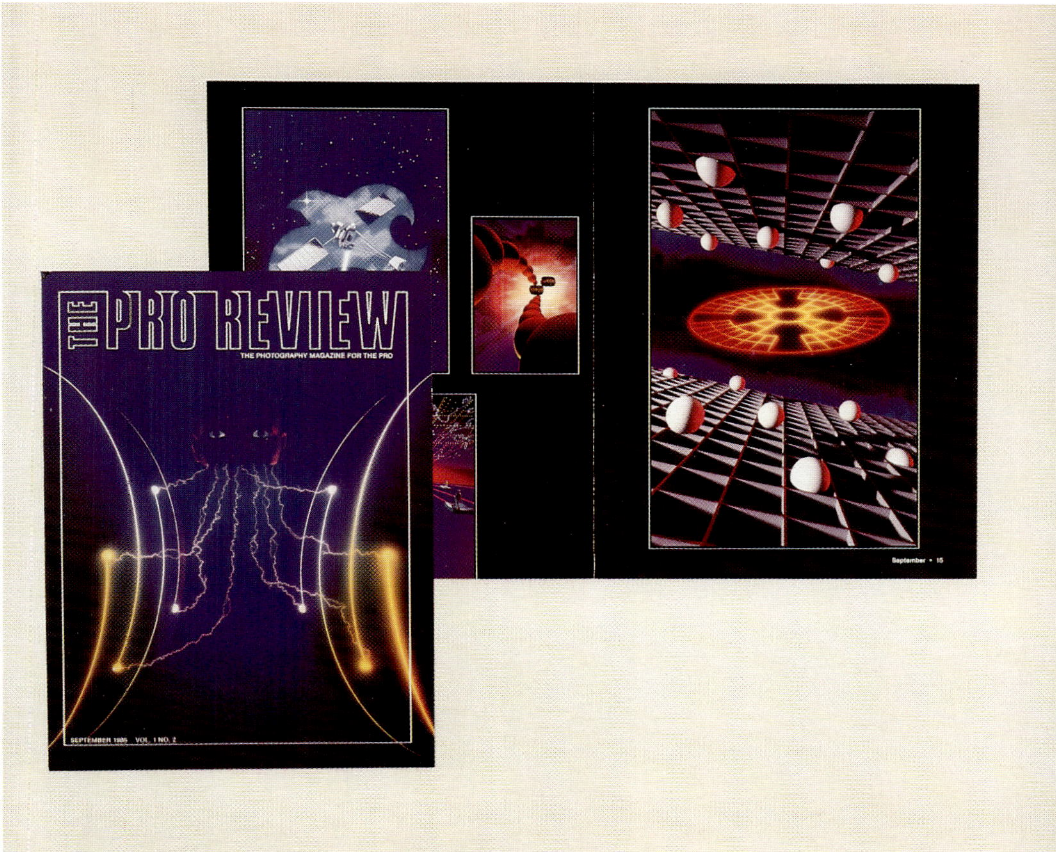

Tcherevkoff's work is spectacular, and he's a natural for coverage by photography magazines. When his work was profiled in *Pro Review*, he wisely ordered reprints of the cover and the article, so that they could be added to the folder.

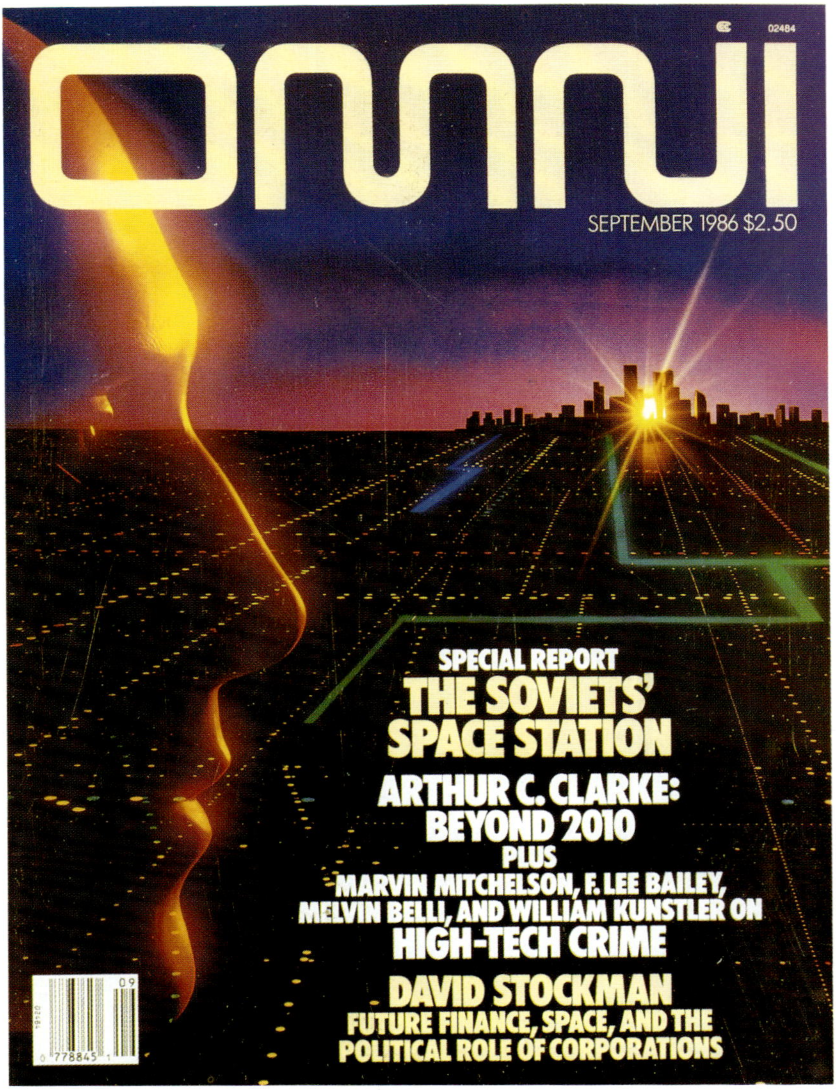

Finally, while Tcherevkoff knows that editorial photography pays less than advertising photography, he regularly shoots covers for *Omni* magazine and then includes the extra tearsheets he receives in his promotion kit.

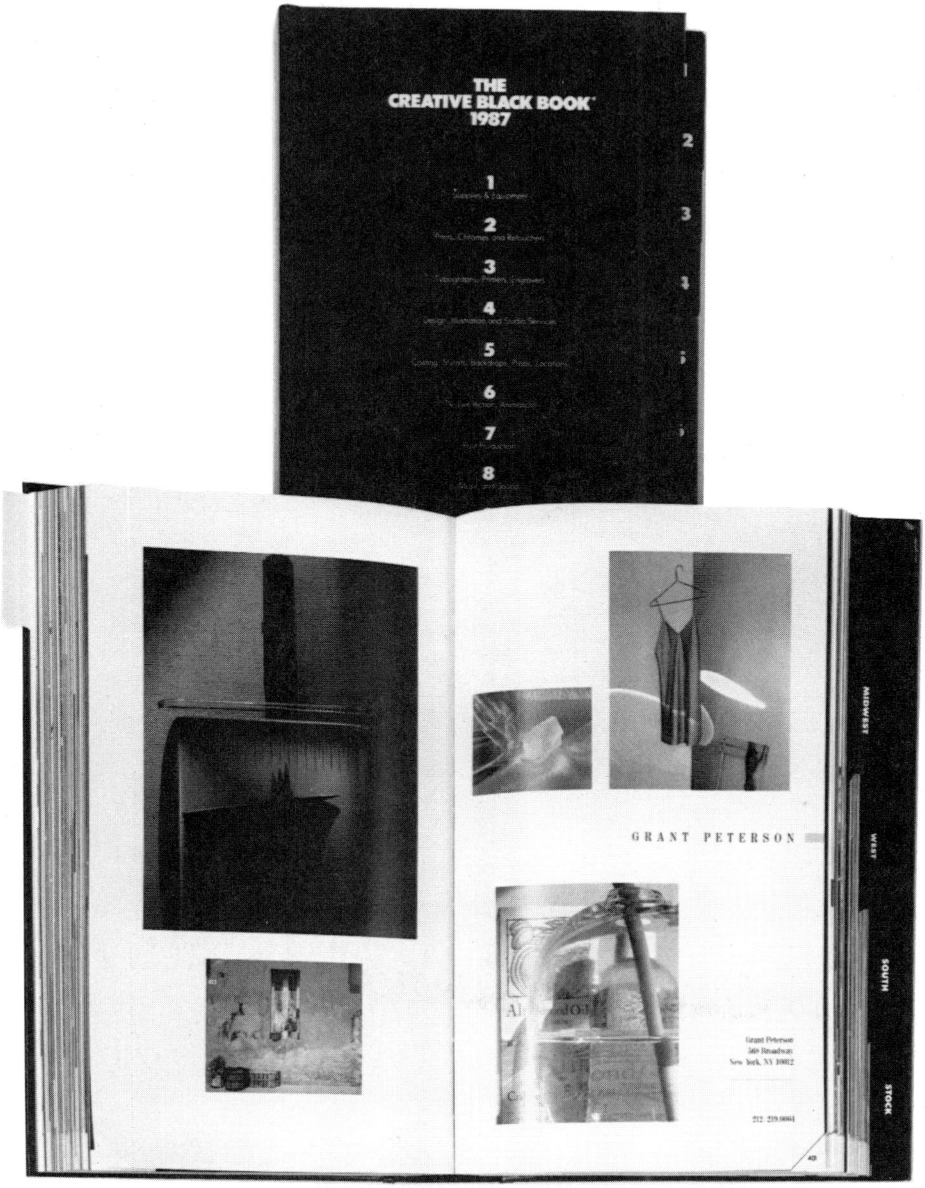

The *Creative Black Book* appears in a two-volume set. Volume One breaks down a listing of suppliers to creative industries, while Volume Two is devoted to page advertising from photographers.

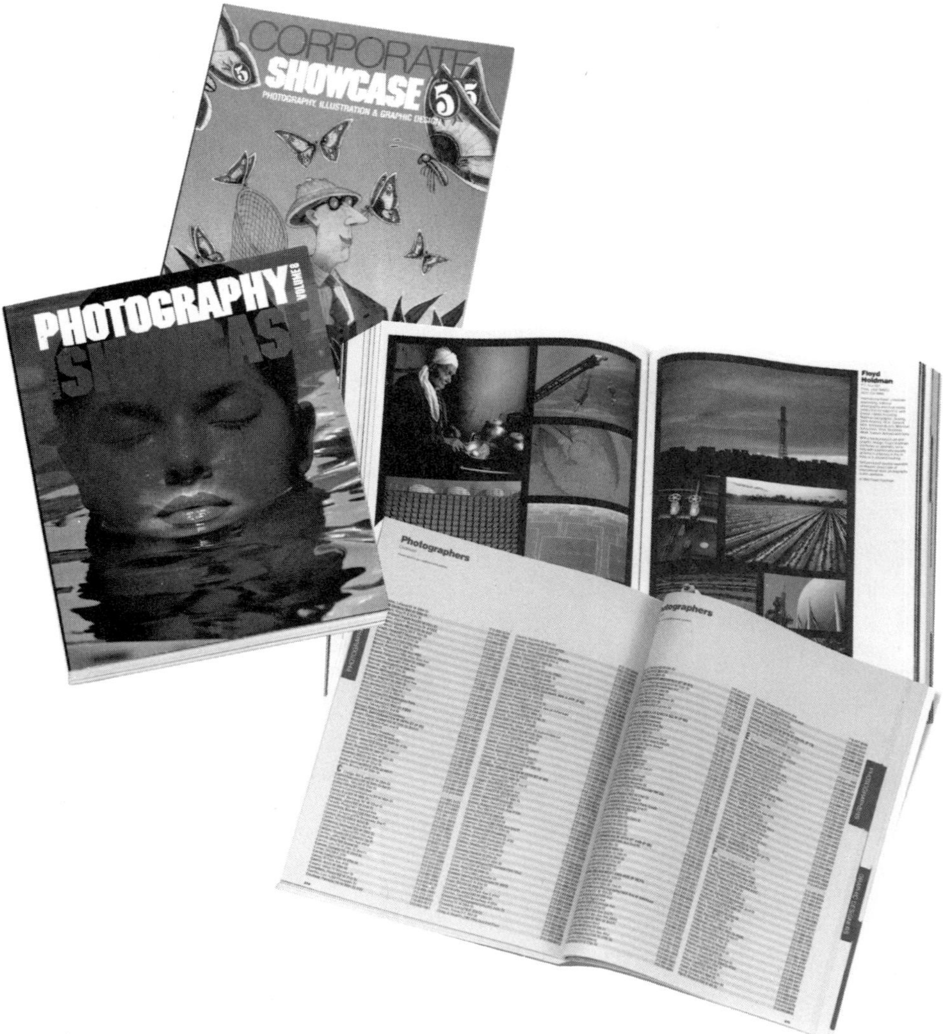

American Showcase offers two directories of interest to photographers: *American Photography Showcase* and *Corporate Showcase*. One of the features of both publications is the "gray pages," in which photographers can list their address and phone number for free.

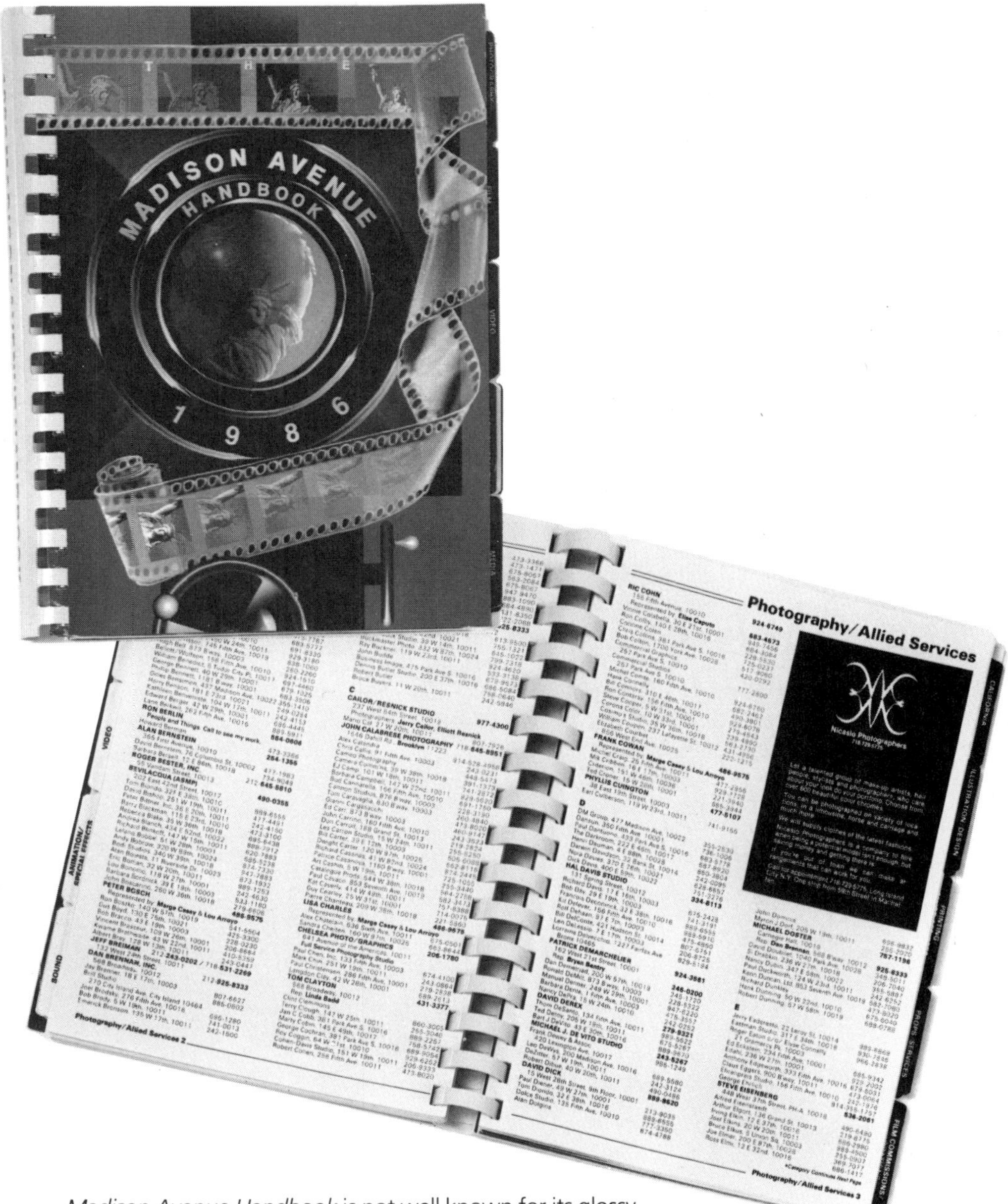

Madison Avenue Handbook is not well known for its glossy full-page advertisements. Most photographers instead choose to simply run a listing with their address and phone number, sometimes referring readers to their larger ads in other directories.

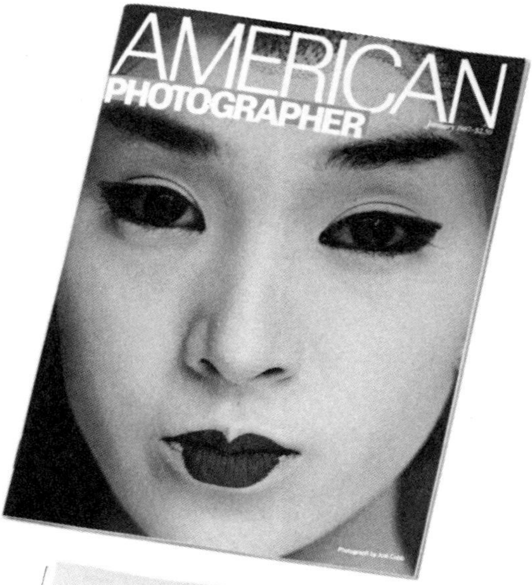

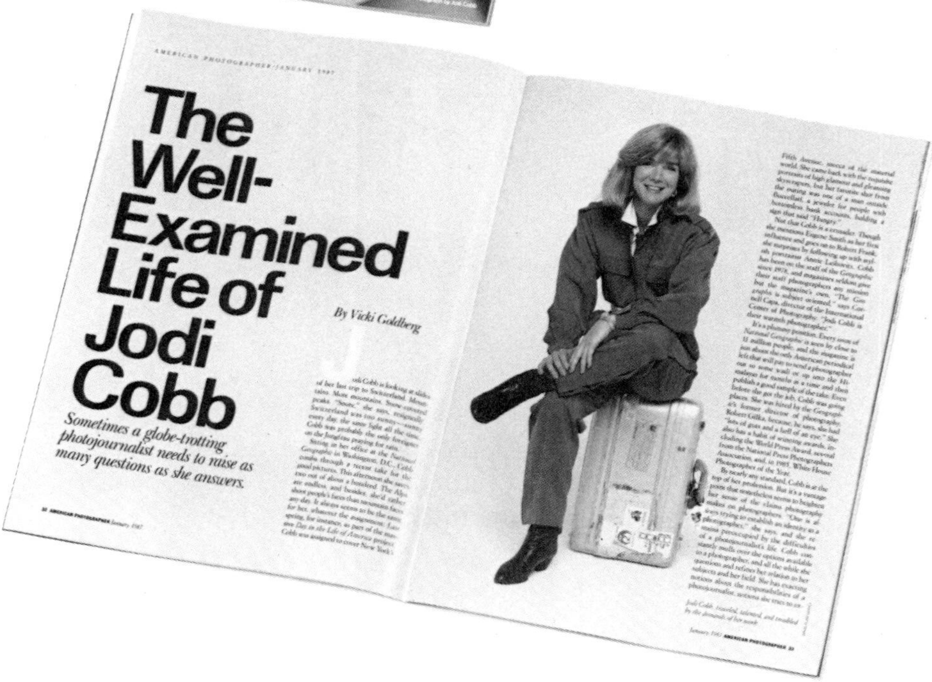
The Well-Examined Life of Jodi Cobb

Sometimes a globe-trotting photojournalist needs to raise as many questions as she answers.

By Vicki Goldberg

Editorial coverage in *American Photographer* is prized by many of the best photographers in the country, making the competition tight, but well worth the effort.

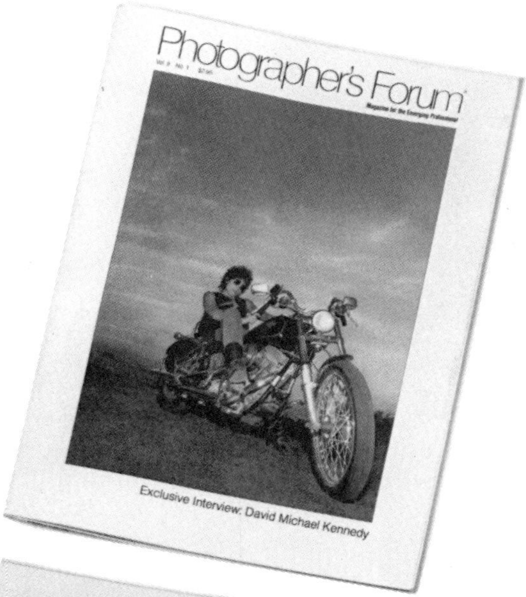

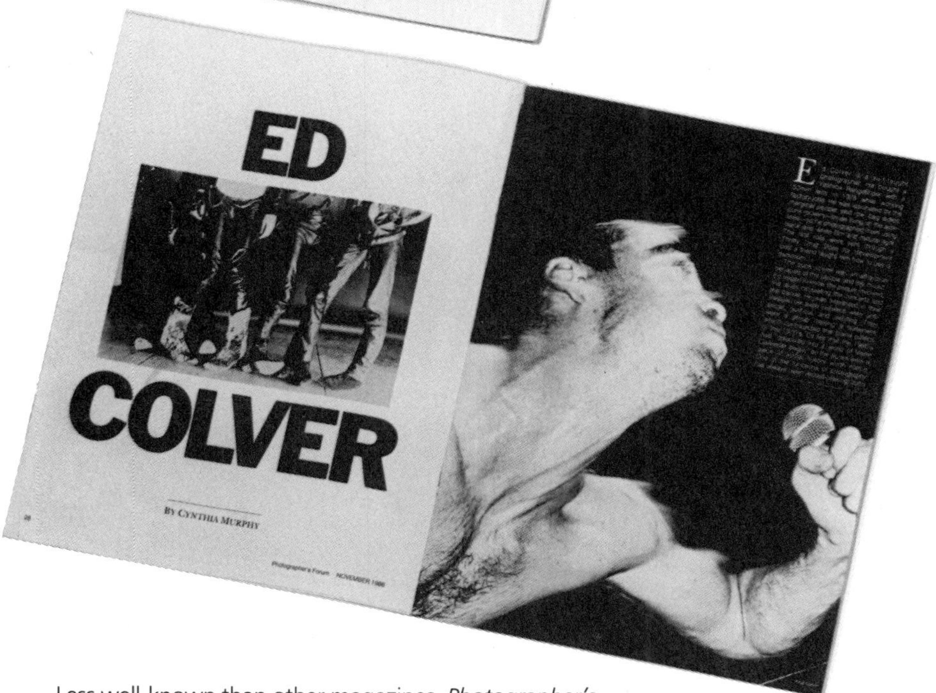

Less well-known than other magazines, *Photographer's Forum* nonetheless features superb design and excellent reproduction. A profile in this publication is a worthy addition to any photographer's list of credits.

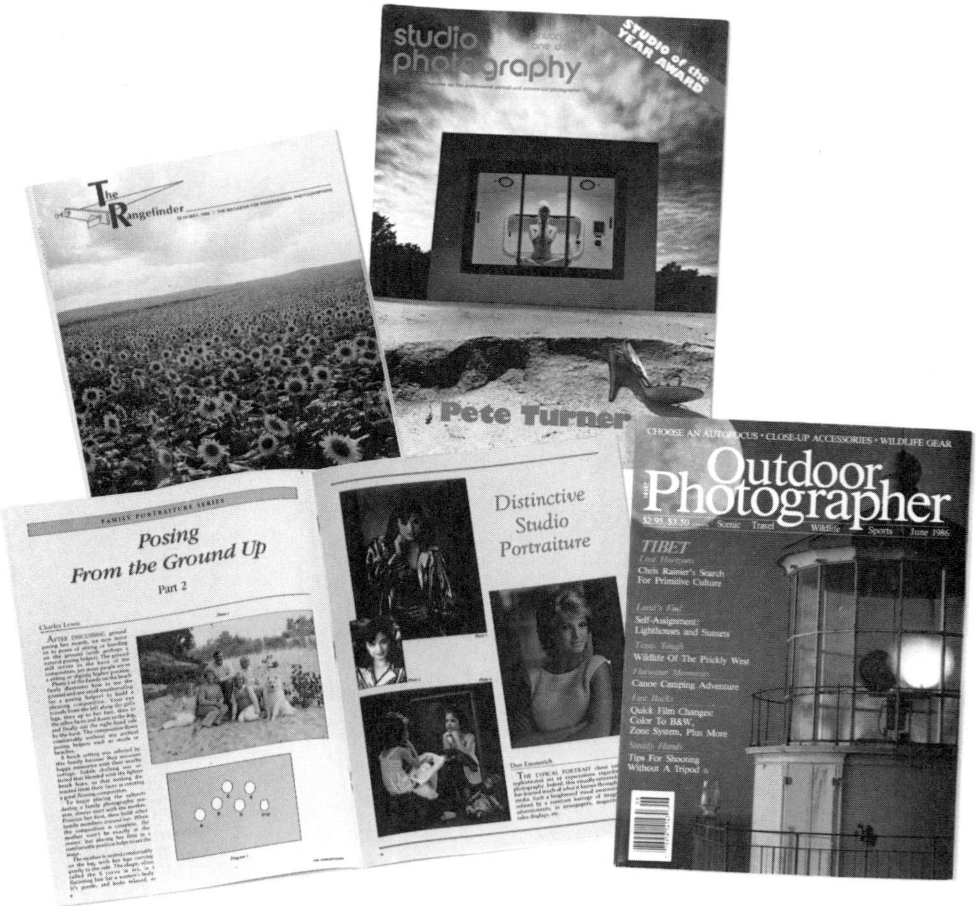

Even in a specialized field such as photography, a variety of magazines abound. Editors are always looking for a photographer who can provide material of interest to their readers.

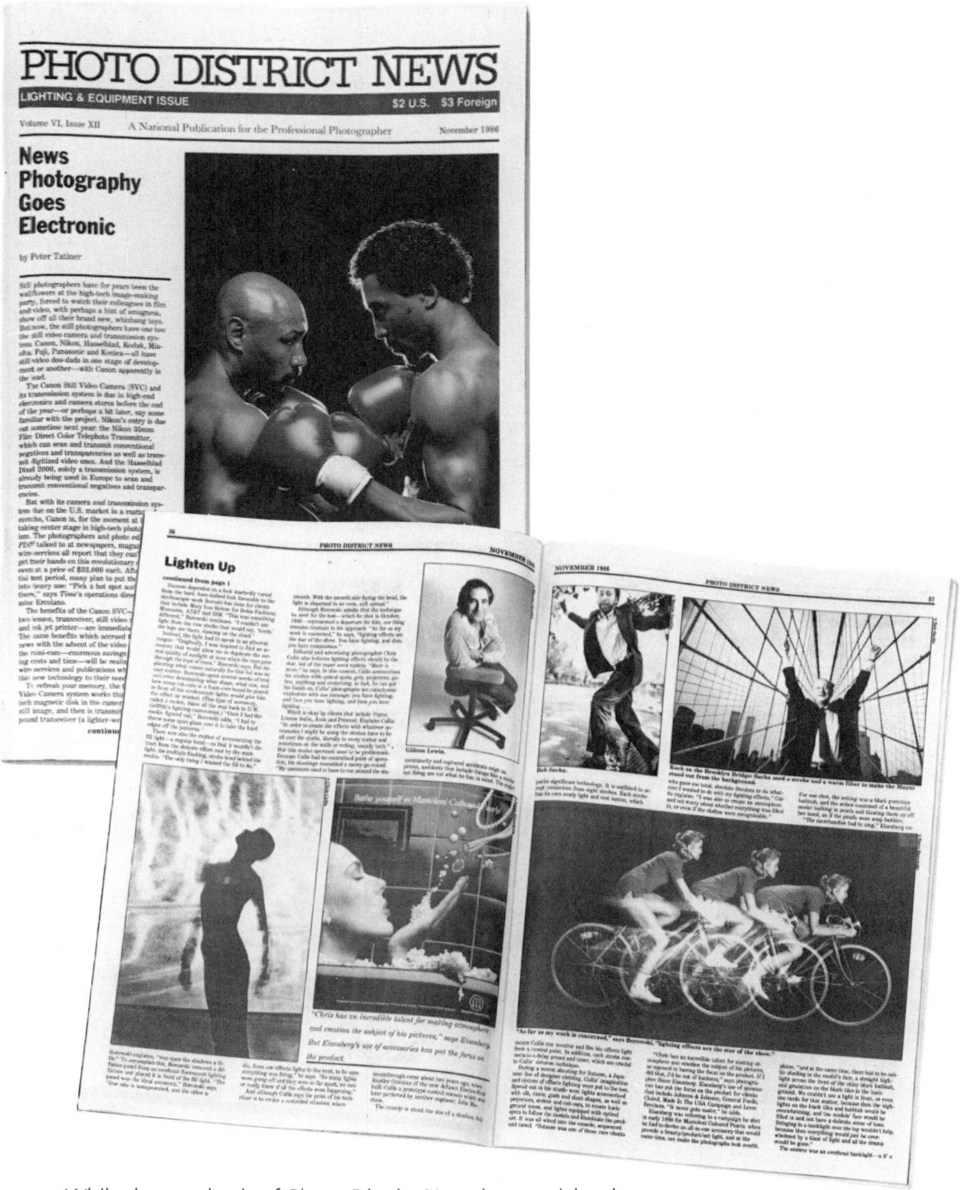

PHOTO DISTRICT NEWS

LIGHTING & EQUIPMENT ISSUE $2 U.S. $3 Foreign

Volume VI, Issue XII A National Publication for the Professional Photographer November 1986

News Photography Goes Electronic

by Peter Tatiner

Still photographers have for years been the wallflowers at the high-tech image-making party, forced to watch their colleagues in film and video, with perhaps a hint of smugness, show off all their brand new, whizbang toys. But now, the still photographers have one too: the still video camera and transmission systems. Canon, Nikon, Hasselblad, Kodak, Minolta, Fuji, Panasonic and Konica—all have still-video doo-dads in one stage of development or another—with Canon apparently in the lead.

The Canon Still Video Camera (SVC) and its transmission system is due in high-end electronics and camera stores before the end of the year—or perhaps a bit later, say some familiar with the project. Nikon's entry is due out sometime next year: the Nikon 35mm Film Direct Color Telephoto Transmitter, which can scan and transmit conventional negatives and transparencies as well as transmit digitized video ones. And the Hasselblad Dixel 2000, solely a transmission system, is already being used in Europe to scan and transmit conventional negatives and transparencies.

PHOTO DISTRICT NEWS

Lighten Up

continued from page 1

"Chris has an incredible talent for making atmosphere and emotion the subject of his pictures," says Eisenberg. But Eisenberg's use of accessories has put the focus on the product.

While the emphasis of *Photo District News* is on articles that are business oriented, profiles of photographers are often published. Because the magazine is printed on newspaper stock, it may not provide the best venue for your photographs, but it's certainly worth the effort to get your name mentioned here.

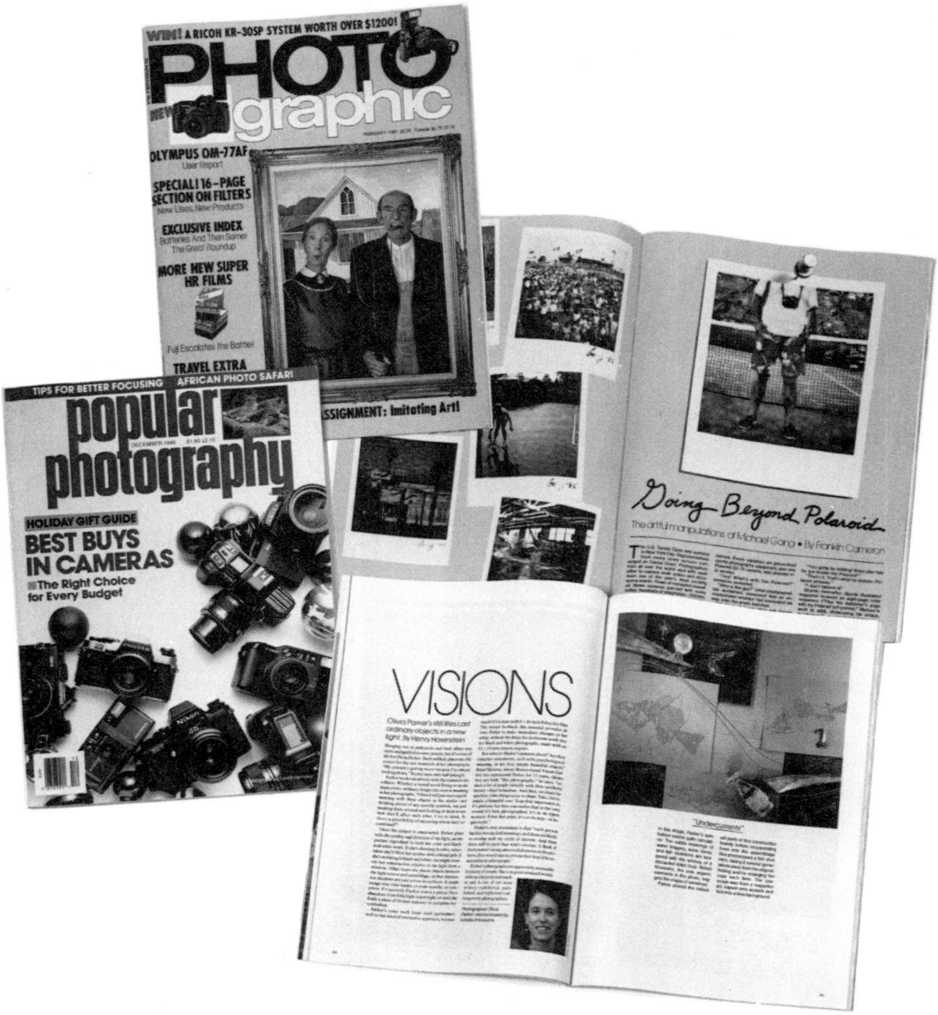

Popular Photography and *Petersen's Photographic* are among the most popular magazines directed toward the amateur market. Editors on the staffs of both publications are open to queries for articles on a wide range of photographic specialties and techniques.

CHAPTER FIVE

The Editorial Connection

Once you're doing paid promotions, it's time to launch the free ones. What I'm about to describe are not "pie-in-the-sky pipe dreams." You can promote yourself with a minimum of money using the elements of free promotion that I'm about to describe.

Why do I have so much confidence in free promotion? Why do I think you can get a layout of your photographs in a magazine, a camera company to promote you, a gallery exhibit, or radio and TV appearances?

The bottom line is that I've worked in all these areas. As a public relations executive for the agency that represented Nikon, Inc., I helped decide which photographers the camera company would promote, booked them on talk shows, and helped decide on which ones got gallery exhibits of their photography. As a photo magazine editor, I published many, many portfolios. As a photographer, I've gotten my photography published in major magazines. As a free-lance writer, I've interviewed and provided the vehicle for publicity to many more professional "shooters." So when I talk about free publicity, I speak from first-hand, intimate knowledge.

Do you know what all the photographers I've known, who wound up using free promotion to their advantage, had in common? First, they presented a good public image. That's not to say they all dressed in shirts and ties, though that does present a professional image. But they all came off as clean, well-dressed, and attractive people you'd want to talk to and be around.

What about their photography, you may be wondering? Well, some of them were terrific. Most weren't. Most were better than average, some were mediocre and quite a few had little or no talent. But do you know why they all got free publicity?

They weren't afraid to try. They put themselves out there. Quite simply, they made the effort and had enough confidence in themselves, if not in their work, to succeed. And as far as promoting themselves for free, they did succeed. There was no special secret to their success. They just did it.

THE GOAL

Free promotions are designed to reach a mass audience, such as the people who come to a gallery exhibit, or the readers of a photography magazine. You hope that a potential client will see your work and like it enough to either buy some photography from you or hire you to create something special just for him.

This "something special" can be anything from an executive portrait to a product ad that will be published in a mass-market magazine. The easiest and most effective way of reaching a potential client with a free promotion is by getting a photography magazine interested enough in your work that they do an article about you.

SPECIFIC VERSUS GENERAL-INTEREST MAGAZINES

You may be asking why you should be soliciting a photography magazine to cover you, rather than a more general publication with a wider circulation? After all, doesn't a general-interest magazine, like *People* for example, print articles about everyone from politicians to photographers?

Yes they do, but the effort involved in getting a general-interest magazine like *People* to cover you may not be worth the amount of time you have to put in to get them interested in the first place. But a magazine like *Popular Photography* or *The Rangefinder* is already predisposed to doing an article about a photographer. In fact, without such articles, they wouldn't survive, because their readers demand them. For all these reasons, you'll find it a lot easier to get a photography rather than a general-interest magazine to report about you.

AVOIDING THE SLUSH PILE

When a photographer contacts a magazine for the express purpose of getting the magazine to do an article about him, that correspondence usually winds up in the "slush pile."

Every photography magazine editor has a "slush pile." It's often a photography stew; the pot is the editor's desk. On it are combined the following ingredients that photographers have sent in, in no particular order: slide sheets, letters of introduction, article suggestions, color and black-and-white photographs, and pictures of photographers at work in which they look like Indiana Jones searching for the Temple of Doom.

Eventually, the editor will answer every unsolicited correspondence in the "slush pile." Perhaps 95 percent will be rejected, not because their work or ideas are inferior, but because they are just one of many who are writing in and it is always difficult to stand out from the crowd. How can you stand out from the crowd, avoid the "slush pile" and get the odds down, so that you have a reasonable chance of success?

How it Works

An unsolicited query is essentially a presentation of a photographer's credentials. Magazine editors look for the following:

1. A detailed query letter. This letter, no more than one typed, single-spaced page, should highlight an unusual or original aspect of the photographer's work, which will make the editor interested enough to assign the article to a writer.

2. The query should be accompanied by about 40 slides, representative of the photographer's work. *Do not* send prints. It's easier for the editor to just slap the slides on a light box, rather than fumbling to get prints out of cartons, and then find enough room in his already overcrowded office from which to view them.

After you've sent the package, containing query and photographs (be sure to include an envelope with return postage) wait about two weeks and then call the magazine directly. Ask for the editor to whom you addressed the package; this will usually be the executive or senior editor.

When you get him on the phone, introduce yourself and, in a

low-key way, ask him if he's looked at your recent solicitation. If he hasn't, which will probably be the case, tell him you know he's busy, but if he could take the time to look at the presentation and give you an *opinion*, you'd appreciate it.

By asking for an opinion, rather than a straight yes or no, you've created a non-threatening atmosphere. The editor will feel free to look at your work without pressure, and thus be more disposed to accepting it.

Profile or Layout?

Once the editor makes a decision to go ahead with an article, he then has to decide whether to commission a profile or straight, layout-type of article.

A profile is composed of an interview with the photographer, where the reader gets to know him as an individual. Sprinkled throughout the text are insights into his personality and what about his work is especially unusual or creative. This latter piece of information was highlighted, you will recall, in the query letter.

Depending on the space available, the profile also features examples of the photographer's work. This may be composed of the work you sent in with the query, additional slides you later provide, or both.

In contrast to a profile, a layout is composed of very few words and a lot of pictures. There's an introductory blurb about who the photographer is, and then a layout of his pictures, which is sometimes accompanied by captions.

Which is More Valuable? Which is more valuable to you, the profile or the layout? A profile, accompanied by your photographs, is more prestigious. There's an inherent importance in the printed word. Potential clients who read the article will say, "This photographer is important enough that someone thought to write about him."

You also get a chance to explain your work in the profile. But in a layout, the work must stand alone. The reader spends more time examining the photographs, because there is no body copy to compete for his attention.

Whether you wind up being featured in a layout or a profile depends on a number of factors, including how much space is available and how important the editor perceives you and your work to be. Whatever the decision, profile or layout, do not argue with the editor. It's tough enough getting into a magazine, and nobody likes a *prima donna*. You'll get a lot further by being cooperative.

ANOTHER APPROACH

So far, I've described how to contact magazines directly. But there's an easier way. Get the writers who work for these magazines to do the work for you.

Photography magazine writers are always looking for photographers with whom they can work. They get paid not just for profiles, but for putting together layouts as well, where copy that they write forms the blurb at the beginning of the layout. They frequently write the captions as well.

If you can contact the writer and get him interested enough, he will write the query, select the photographs, and submit the package to the magazine. This is a good deal, because the writer will have a direct contact on the magazine to approach—no "slush pile." The contact is an editor he deals with on a regular basis, who listens with open ears.

You can find the writer to take up your cause simply by reading the magazine you're interested in approaching and noting the names of the writers. Then write to them directly, in care of the magazine, and ask them if they'd like to approach the magazine on your behalf. Be sure to enclose a stamped, self-addressed envelope for a response.

A CASE STUDY

Wyman Meinzer is one of the best examples I can recall of a photographer who understands the editorial process and used that knowledge to get a profile and layout of his work in photo magazines.

Meinzer is a wildlife photographer, based in Benjamin, Texas, a small town about 120 miles east of Lubbock. What makes Meinzer so unique is that he used to be a trapper, trapping animals and then selling their pelts. Today, he uses that knowledge to stalk the little critters and when he's close enough, take extremely naturalistic shots with his 35mm SLR.

The other factor that makes Meinzer unique is that he flies his own plane, spotting the wildlife from the air. He then lands the plane and trucks to the location to take his photographs.

Meinzer began his "editorial connection" by managing to contact a local newspaper, which did an article about him. Keep in mind that newspaper articles are only in the public eye a very short time, one day in fact, as opposed to magazine articles which are on the stands at least a month. But in Meinzer's case, that one day was enough.

In the course of the interview, Meinzer mentioned that he used Canon equipment. Now, every camera company has a clipping service, which is always on the lookout for product mention in print. When they saw the name Canon in the Meinzer article, the clipping was forwarded to The Rowland Company, the public relations agency that represents Canon.

There, the account supervisor on the Canon account (at the time, Lyman Gaylord) read the piece and was impressed enough with Meinzer's story to contact me. He knew I was looking for an interesting photographer to profile and figured Meinzer would be right up my alley. He sent me the clipping. After reading it, I contacted Meinzer and told him I wanted to do an article about him.

"Sounds like a fine idea, Fred," he said over the phone, in a heavy Texas accent that made Fred sound like "Frid."

Subsequently, I did a phone interview with Meinzer and wrote a brief profile for The Rangefinder, *but I wasn't satisfied. I felt the story* needed to have a little more depth, which would require my visiting with Meinzer in person.

I submitted a query to my editor at Popular Photography, Steve Pollock, which he liked. When I went in to show him the pictures, he wasn't enamored. He felt that Meinzer was a little weak in visual design and that the slides were dirty. Remember, presentation is important too.

After thinking about it, Steve said: "Fred, this is a close call, but I have to pass."

At this point, I'd already invested a lot of time in writing the proposal and presenting it. I could have abandoned it. After all, I'd already done the article for The Rangefinder. But I really liked Meinzer's story and while his photographs weren't the best of the genre, there was a harsh beauty to them. I felt he deserved more of a say and I wanted to tell his story.

I went back to Meinzer and told him that Pollock's criticism of the slides' physical presentation was justified. He sent me a spanking new set, and I next approached Connoisseur magazine. After stalling for six months, they assigned me the piece and paid my expenses down to Texas, where I interviewed Meinzer, went up in the plane with him, then into the field for the photo session. Before I left, I picked out some more shots for illustration.

What Connoisseur had in mind was a combination profile and layout. The photographs would be on separate pages, away from the copy.

Then, a hitch developed. Where Popular Photography had trouble with the photographs, Connoisseur's editors had trouble with Meinzer's personal history. Even though the original query stated that Meinzer was no longer a trapper, they found his past involvement objectionable enough to cancel the article.

Meinzer and I were both disappointed, but rather than let things go, I decided to make one more stab and Meinzer agreed.

The photographs, along with the article that had originally been prepared for Connoisseur, were sent to Outdoor Photographer. This is a photography magazine that specializes in publishing articles about landscape and wildlife photographers. This time, we were a hit.

The publisher and editor Steve Werner liked the package. He published the article and had a special section within it, much like

Connoisseur *had contemplated, featuring Meinzer's photographs.*

I think this story amply illustrates how the "editorial connection" works. Of course, not every photographer has as unique a story to tell as Wyman Meinzer, nor photographs as dramatic. But the reason I went to bat for him over such a long period of time was because he's a nice guy. That to me, and most writers and editors, is more important than the photographer's talent. Combine talent with an even disposition and you have an unbeatable combination that even the most cynical editors and writers cannot turn down.

Following is the article about Wyman Meinzer, but not as published. I've made certain editorial changes for the sake of timeliness. While reading it, pay attention to how well Meinzer comes off. That's because I liked him, not just as a photographer but as a person.

After reading it, go back and substitute yourself for Meinzer. Think about what points you'd like to see emphasized about you and your business in a profile, and how you would use the subsequent article for promotional purposes.

That Extra Half a Second, by Frederic W. Rosen

"That rattlesnake is just waiting for me to come within that extra half-inch, so he can lash out and kill me. He's flicking out that tongue, sensing my body heat. When I'm close enough, he'll strike. Then I take the photograph."

For 34-year-old wildlife photographer Wyman Meinzer, taking photographs is a matter of calculated risks. He has to make sure he's that extra half-inch away from the rattler's fangs. Otherwise, he's dead.

"When I see an animal, my first impulse is to get my gun. But instead, I get my camera." Indeed, Meinzer has to reconcile two opposing facets of his personality: hunter and photographer.

Meinzer's father, a ranch foreman, raised his son in the savage parts of north Texas and taught him to hunt in order to survive. Meinzer later earned a degree in wildlife management at Texas Tech University, but after graduation he couldn't find any jobs in his chosen field. Where some people in a similar predicament might have become waiters or shoe salesmen to make ends meet, Meinzer decided to become a professional hunter of bobcat and coyote, creatures that can be a menace to both man and animal alike.

Hunting the Texas outback—Crocodile Dundee would be at home out there—a deep-seated conflict eventually surfaced. Trained to search and destroy, Meinzer now felt his long-held appreciation for the animals' beauty vying for a louder voice.

One moonlit night, he read through some wildlife magazines, taking particular interest in the pictures. "I remember thinking, 'Why can't *I* become a wildlife photographer and use a camera to communicate my feelings of what it's like to be with the animals in the wild?' "

Meinzer traded his gun for a Canon camera and began taking pictures. Through trial and error, he discovered which ones sold. John Nuhn, the art director for *International Wildlife*, a magazine to which Meinzer frequently contributes, says, "Wyman's photographs don't stand out like those of a person who's had a lot of design courses. It's the hunting techniques he employs, coupled with a natural talent for photography, that make his work aesthetically pleasing."

Meinzer explains how he uses his experience as a hunter to photograph a jack rabbit in a field of wildflowers:

"I sit and let the jack rabbit see me. If I try and sneak up on him, and he hasn't seen me and then looks up, it's all over. So I let him see me. I stand there and slowly sit down, so he gets used to the change in height. He stares at me for ten minutes, but eventually, he gets used to me. Then he turns around and starts scratching. That's when I move.

"I crawl toward him on my belly, careful not to make any loud noises or abrupt movements. I slide further along until I'm at least 30 yards away. I stop and start photographing with my Canon F-1 35mm SLR and 600mm telephoto lens. Because the lens has a shallow depth-of-field, I'm able to isolate the jack rabbit, or any subject, in a central, crystal-clear portion of the frame."

In a Meinzer photograph, you will never see an animal that's easy to shoot, because it doesn't offer a challenge. Instead, Meinzer has made a decision to create rare, realistic images of animals in their own environment. Despite the dangers that are sometimes inherent in his work, Meinzer will get close enough to an animal so you, the viewer, may see the expression on its face and recognize it as an *individual* among its species.

How does Meinzer manage to get into the wild to take his photographs? He takes to the air to spot the wildlife, then lands and trucks inland to photograph them.

Off Texas State Highway 20, outside Meinzer's hometown of Benjamin, is a long, narrow blacktop that serves as an airstrip. Parked alongside it is a 1948 two-seater airplane, which Meinzer and his passenger push out onto the runway. With the plane pointed in the right direction, Meinzer curls his tall, rawboned frame into the front seat, while his passenger does the same in the back. The door is off, so Meinzer can easily spot his quarry.

"Contact!" Meinzer pushes some buttons and the propeller comes to life. When it hits top speed, Meinzer lets out the throttle with his left hand, then grabs the control stick with his right. The plane taxis down the runway, picks up speed, and is finally lifted into the sky by the air rushing under the wings and the engine's revs.

It's a calm day, the air as smooth as glass. Meinzer climbs higher and banks inland. He leans out the open door, searching for coyote or other wildlife indigenous to the area. He motions toward a flock of wild turkey below, makes a mental note of their location and heads back.

Flying over a power line, Meinzer sees the airstrip rapidly coming into view. He eases forward on the stick and the plane sinks. Within moments, the three wheels touch the blacktop and the plane lands softly. He taxis it to the end of the runway where his battered Datsun pick-up is waiting.

After the plane is tied down, Meinzer and his passenger hop into the vehicle. He heads six miles inland, toward the position of the wild turkey. It is only 7 AM.

"I only shoot early in the morning," he says. "The light is softer and truer than at any other time of day. Dawn's light really brings out nature's true colors. The greens and reds in the hills are rich and deep. This is the type of saturated color that is necessary to make a great photograph."

Reaching his destination, Meinzer stops the truck just as the wild turkey flee in single file down a dry creek bed. Grabbing his camera, he runs after them, leaping unscathed over a barbed wire fence and out-distancing his passenger in seconds. Soon, Meinzer emerges from the brush 1000 yards away.

"Move to your left. We'll flush 'em out," he yells. His passenger does as instructed, seeing nothing. Suddenly, in front of him, are the wild turkey. They are running toward Meinzer. When they are within 30 feet of him, they leap into the air and Meinzer lets loose with his motor-driven camera.

"I think I got a good shot of a turkey flying," he says afterward. "You know, when I was younger, all I could think about was knocking the heck out of the animals. But as I get older, with every picture I take, I'm trying to capture that animal in its most beautiful state, exactly the way I see it in the wild. I want the viewer to look at my photograph of a wild turkey, for instance, and say, 'My God, I never knew that animal could be so beautiful.' "

WHAT TO SAY WHEN INTERVIEWED

Once the writer has been assigned the story, he'll be contacting you to arrange an interview. Depending on his schedule, and the area of the country in which he lives, he'll talk to you either on the phone or in person.

If possible, try to see him personally. Personal interviews always come out better because nothing beats that emotional immediacy. If not, and the interview is done on the phone, try to make your answers as direct as possible. The writer will probably be recording what you say and you'll make his job easier if he doesn't have to wade through a lot of garbled answers to get to the core of what you're saying.

Whether it's a phone or in-person interview, make sure you've set aside the time to talk. This will give the writer the opportunity to get behind the natural defenses we all have when someone talks to us, especially about our work.

Be honest in answering questions. That doesn't mean you have to completely expose your soul, but the reader will know if you're giving a "rap," rather than honest answers.

I can think of one instance where I interviewed a fashion photographer who told me that his work expressed, ". . . the spiritual nature of the existential elements of my gypsy background." I swear, he actually said that. When I told him I didn't understand, he put a hurt and confused look on his face, and then started with the spiritual speech again. I was never satisfied with that article because the photographer hadn't been honest.

When the interview is over, ask the writer if you can take a look at his copy for "technical corrections." Most magazines usually do not allow the photographer to do this. But if you're not asking for copy approval (which you won't get anyway) and all you want to do is make technical corrections," there's a chance your request will be granted.

By offering your "technical corrections," in reality you're controlling the flow of information in the article. In essence, what you're trying to do is direct the writer to write about the facets of you and your work that will help promote your photography to prospective clients.

As I said, the odds are against getting this type of control. So, hedge your bet during the interview itself. Tell the writer what you'd like to see in print and why. Again, I can't state too strongly that this honesty, despite it being self-serving, will be respected by the writer and editor, rather than phony responses.

FOLLOW UP

After the interview is over, ask the writer when the article is scheduled to run. Most magazines have a lead time—the time it takes to put an issue together for publication—that's anywhere from one to three months, and sometimes longer. If you have a gallery exhibit, new account breaking in print, or something of that nature occurring at the time when the article is supposed to be published, make sure you mention this to the writer *at the time of the interview*. It gives him a timely publication "hook" that will lessen the chance of a publication delay and provide you with an article that is much more of a promotional tool, because you're using it to promote something specific.

Call the writer once a month after the interview has been completed, as you continue to check on scheduling. Sometimes, articles will be pushed back, despite timely "hooks," but if you let the writer know you're alive, he'll push for publication. Why? Because many times in the photo magazine business, the writer isn't paid for his work until the article sees print. The sooner it's published, the sooner he gets paid.

ILLUSTRATING THE ARTICLE

Provide photographs to illustrate the article at the time of the interview. It's too easy to shunt this aside for another day and before you know it, you're causing delays.

Articles cannot be printed without pictures in the editor's office, whether they're used or not. The editor wants and needs that option. It's to your benefit to provide photographs as soon as possible.

Magazines prefer transparencies. They can also work with prints, and they have to in the case of black-and-white photography, but slides are the preferred format.

Make sure that the slides you present for publication are not dupes. Magazines always have trouble getting accurately registered color reproductions from their printers. Removing one generation from the process only complicates things, so provide originals.

After the writer has picked out the images from your stock to illustrate the article, make sure that he signs an invoice, indicating that he is taking the photographs for publication in the magazine he represents. This way, if the slides are misplaced or destroyed, you have some paperwork to indicate that you gave them to the writer in the first place.

PAYMENT

Magazines do not pay photographers to interview them. However, many do pay for the use of their photographs.

Payment breaks down in two ways: by picture and by page rate. Sometimes, you can negotiate with the editor for a package price for your photographs, but in general they adhere to one of the two picture-payment policies just mentioned.

CONSUMER AND TRADE MAGAZINES

As stated earlier, consumer magazines, like *Popular Photography*, are sold on the stands and by subscription. They reach a large, mass audience. Trade magazines, like *The Rangefinder*, are distributed free-of-charge by mail to much more of a specific audience, namely other professional photographers. Their circulation is also lower than the consumer magazines.

Both types of magazines usually have art directors at ad agencies on their mailing lists, as well as other potential clients, like photo galleries. So there is value to getting coverage in either type of publication. However, because of their larger circulation, and the prestige associated with being published in them, consumer magazines are the preferred medium for your layout or profile.

Correspondingly, because photographers desire publication more in the consumer than trade magazines, competition is that much keener. If you are a photographer who is just beginning his quest for the "editorial connection," it would be wise to set your sights high and query the consumer magazines first. But if you are rejected, immediately go to the trade magazines, where you have a better chance of breaking in. As you progress in your photographic career, and people begin to know your work and reputation, it will be easier to break into the consumer magazines.

TEARSHEETS

Once your layout or profile has been published, ask the magazine for tearsheets, as many as you can get. Your use of these tearsheets is two-fold:

1. *Laminate* a set and keep them in your permanent portfolio. Show them to a prospective client when trying to clinch a job.

2. Send the tearsheets, which have been carefully trimmed of ragged edges, to a select group of prospective clients you really have a shot at getting. Editorial coverage is always impressive. Follow up with a phone call to the prospective client to discuss the article and simply ask if they liked it. Then, lead the conversation around to a discussion of the job you want to shoot.

AN ANALYSIS

There are many photography magazines published and it's difficult figuring out who publishes what and which ones you should approach.

In the following list, I've broken down both trade and photography consumer magazines. I've listed them according to the importance I feel they will have in promoting your photography.

Each listing contains an analysis of the editorial content of each magazine. Included is the name of the *editorial position* to which you should direct your queries.

I have not listed the name of the individuals currently assuming those positions, because the publishing world is a volatile one and editors frequently change jobs. What does remain constant is the editorial position at each magazine in charge of responding to queries.

To get the name of the person currently holding the position indicated, simply call the magazine. When you get the switchboard say, "Please give me the name of the senior editor (for example)." That is the name of the person to whom you address your query.

TRADE MAGAZINES

PHOTO/DESIGN
1 Park Avenue
New York, NY 10016
(212) 685-8520

Address all queries to the Editor

Photo/Design *is a high-class trade journal. Perhaps because of this, it is the only trade magazine to charge for a subscription. Because the magazine is designed to and does reach many ad agency art directors, its pages are full of* Creative-Black-Book- *and* American-Showcase-*style advertisements by photographers, especially those working in the commercial areas.*

Photo/Design *publishes both profiles and layouts with sumptuous detail to reproduction of photographs. For this reason, and its ability to target and reach a specific audience that regularly hires photographers for jobs, I place* Photo/Design *at the top of this list.*

THE RANGEFINDER
1312 Lincoln Blvd.
Santa Monica, CA 90406
(213) 451-8506

Address all queries to the Editor

The Rangefinder is designed to reach professional photographers specializing in wedding, portrait, and industrial work.

The editorial content is a carefully thought-out mix of business articles, and profiles and layouts of a photographer's work. The profiles and layouts usually run toward wedding and portrait photographers, but the magazine is eclectic and will also publish articles about commercial, wildlife, underwater, and other types of photographers.

The Rangefinder, *like all trade magazines, is in existence to sell advertising to equipment manufacturers. Perhaps because of the advertisers' insistence on getting their ads reproduced correctly, the quality carries over into the editorial area. Great pains are taken to ensure that a photographer's work is reproduced accurately.*

THE PROFESSIONAL PHOTOGRAPHER

1090 Executive Way
Des Plaines, IL 60018
(312) 299-8161

Address all queries to the Editor

The Professional Photographer *is published by the Professional Photographers of America (PPA). The magazine is strictly for wedding and portrait photographers. Its editorial content includes business and technical articles. Profiles and layouts are limited to wedding and portrait photographers.*

Because the magazine does not pay contributors, most professional writers won't do profiles for them and consequently the articles leave a lot to be desired. But while The Professional Photographer *might be guilty of parsimony, the reproduction of its photographs is, like the previous two magazines on the list, excellent. For this reason, I think it's a great place for wedding and portrait photographers to get a layout of their photographs.*

STUDIO PHOTOGRAPHY

Crossways Park West
Woodbury, NY 11797
(212) 895-8370

Address all queries to the Managing Editor

On the plus side, Studio Photography *does a good job of bringing a variety of features to its readers, who are mostly wedding and portrait photographers, with a smattering of commercial and industrial photographers thrown in. The features include business and technical articles. Profiles and layouts of just about every type of photographer are published, though wedding and portrait photographers are emphasized.*

Also on the plus side, Studio Photography *has given profiles and layouts to many professional photographers, especially those at the beginning or intermediate stages of their careers. But the down side is that the magazine's art direction in terms of layout and color reproductions ranges from fair to poor.*

None of which means you shouldn't query Studio Photography; *some press is always better than no press. I just think you'll have to be a little more forceful in conveying to the writer and editor that you're a skilled professional, who won't have his work treated in a cavalier manner. If they take exception to this statement, then walk. There are still a lot of magazines I haven't covered yet.*

PHOTO DISTRICT NEWS

167 Third Avenue
New York, NY 10003
(212) 677-8418

Address all queries to the Editor

Photo District News *is actually a monthly newspaper, published in tabloid format. The newspaper now features regional sections in the national edition, which are geared toward the different sections of the United States.*

The editorial emphasis is placed on helping the photographer become a better businessman, so most of the articles are business oriented. There are also profiles of photographers who are doing something interesting or have used some sort of technique to advance their business.

I put Photo District News *at the bottom of this list for two reasons: one, the newspaper is printed, with the exception of its cover and selected advertisements, on a newspaper-style stock, which is not conducive to vivid or accurate reproduction of photographs; and two, the magazine has a* very *limited circulation, despite its regional sections.*

However, despite these negatives, or perhaps because of them, it is a place where you can get a profile. The newspaper has a lot of pages to fill up each issue and is always looking for articles. In addition, it's received by ad agency art directors, so you might want to consider it.

CONSUMER MAGAZINES

AMERICAN PHOTOGRAPHER

1515 Broadway
New York, NY 10036
(212) 719-6279

Address all queries to the Editor, Sean Callahan

Despite a minuscule staff, when compared to the other consumer magazines, American Photographer *is, quite simply, the best photography magazine published in the United States. I don't know any photographer who doesn't want to have a profile or layout in the magazine.*

It's going to be rather difficult to break in here, because you'll be competing with just about every other photographer in the country. You'll need an excellent query and a cracker-jack photographic presentation.

If you do get published in American Photographer, *it will give your career a considerable boost. Not only is it the most prestigious photo magazine in the country, read by major art directors, you will be able to take considerable pride in knowing that you've succeeded where many, many other photographers failed.*

POPULAR PHOTOGRAPHY

1 Park Avenue
New York, NY 10016
(212) 503-3724

Address all queries to the Executive Editor

Popular Photography *is the preeminent magazine for the amateur and advanced-amateur photographer.*

There's a preponderance of how-to articles in its pages, most of which are written by staffers, while illustrations are supplied by the magazine's staff or submitted by photographers like yourself. Each issue usually features one profile, layout, or both.

You have a good shot at getting some sort of coverage in Popular Photography. *The staff, many of whom are professional photographers, has always been particularly open to queries, and publication in this magazine also carries with it a certain prestige. It is widely read by ad agency art directors, gallery owners, and others in a position to hire photographers.*

PHOTOGRAPHER'S FORUM

25 W. Anapamu
Santa Barbara, CA 93101
(805) 963-0439

Address all queries to the Editor

Photographer's Forum *is a magazine that is mainly designed for students of photography, who comprise a large part of the readership. But the magazine is also sold on newsstands, especially those that stock "art" publications.*

I've listed this magazine third, despite its small circulation, precisely because it is an "art" book. The profiles and layouts are sumptuously done. Great care is taken to produce well-written and edited articles, along with vivid reproductions of photographs.

Because many photographers never even think to query Photographer's Forum *when launching an editorial promotion, the competition to get in here is not as fierce as the previous two listings. You'll find that a profile or layout here will make a worthy addition to your portfolio.*

PETERSEN'S PHOTOGRAPHIC

8490 Sunset Boulevard
Los Angeles, CA 90069
(213) 854-2222

Address all queries to the Senior Editor

This magazine regularly publishes profiles and layouts, in addition to the usual technical and how-to articles, making it an excellent place in which to get coverage.

MODERN PHOTOGRAPHY
825 Seventh Avenue
New York, NY 10019
(212) 265-8360

Address all queries to the Senior Editor

Even though Modern Photography *is neck-and-neck with* Popular Photography *as the most widely used photography magazine, I've listed it this far down on the list for two reasons.*

First and foremost, it publishes few layouts and profiles. Second, the magazine leans heavily toward using its own staff to illustrate the how-to and equipment review articles that make up 95 percent of its editorial content.

Your best chance of getting in here is to query the magazine on a how-to article that is illustrated with your own photographs.

OUTDOOR PHOTOGRAPHER
16200 Ventura Blvd.
Encino, CA 91436
(818) 986-8400

Address all queries to the Managing Editor

Outdoor Photographer *specializes in layouts and profiles of photographers who shoot landscapes and wildlife. There's also a potpourri of technical and how-to articles.*

If you specialize in shooting outdoors, this magazine is ideal for you. They are receptive to publishing first-timers, but only as long as your photographs show your professional accomplishments.

However, this magazine has a big drawback: it can wait as long as a year to publish your work, which means you wait a year to get paid!

NETWORKING CONTACTS

If you follow the advice and promotional techniques I have thus far advanced, you will break into print and, eventually, have a profile and/or layout which you can use to promote yourself.

Specifically, I've talked about promotion through contact with editors and writers by letter. There's another way to make contact with these people. This time, it's done over cocktails.

When a camera company is introducing a new product, it invites representatives of all the magazines listed to press conferences. Over cocktails and lunch, the photography editors and writers socialize, exchange ideas, and discuss the equipment they are there to see introduced.

These press conferences are an excellent place for the photographer interested in promoting himself to meet these people, network contacts, and wind up with editorial coverage. The hitch is getting invited.

The easiest way to get on the invitation lists is to sell a small technical article to one of the magazines listed. Then, call up the public relations agencies that represent the camera companies (see next chapter) and ask them to add your name to the press lists as a freelance writer. Most will gladly oblige. I know of at least five photographers who did this and wound up making editorial contacts at the press conferences, which later led to profiles, layouts, regular columns, and staff positions.

Another way of getting on the lists is if you have a store-front photography studio in which you also sell equipment. Usually, it's large wholesalers who are invited to the conferences, but if you build yourself up over the phone when talking to those in charge of compiling the press lists (usually the secretaries at the PR agencies), you should be able to get yourself invited.

A third way is to tell these same people that you're a prominent photographer, always interested in their client's products—which you regularly purchase. It helps if you actually use the particular camera company's product. It'll make you sound that much more convincing and increase your chances of getting invited.

CHAPTER SIX

Galleries and Other Exhibit Areas

The second major form of free self-promotion is an exhibit of your work. Usually this takes place in a photography gallery.

THE PURPOSE

For the photographer on the way up, a gallery exhibit is an excellent vehicle for introducing your work to potential clients. As part of the promotion of the exhibit, gallery owners send out invitations to people they want to attend, usually regular customers and members of the media who review shows or can do articles about exhibiting photographers and their work. You supply the gallery with your own list of people to invite. Foremost on that list are the names of present clients and potential clients. Present clients will be impressed with the fact that you have your own show. Potential clients might be impressed enough with the work to hire you to shoot some jobs.

The already established photographer has a different goal for a gallery exhibit. As an established photographer, you might be locked into a certain style that clients expect you to use, and they don't think you're capable of anything else. No matter how much the client is paying you, this is a stifling situation.

By having a gallery show of new work that employs a different style or unusual subjects, you get an opportunity to stretch and show what you're really capable of doing. It may induce the client to let you shoot jobs in a different way, or it may not. But you will have started telling people through your work that you are not to be stereotyped, that you're capable of more than what they are used to seeing.

Word of Mouth

Word of mouth is ephemeral, intangible, and impossible to measure, but it definitely exists. When people go to see an exhibit and they like it, they talk about it. This word of mouth builds an audience, especially where one didn't exist before. If an exhibit gets "hot," the word filters down to the right people, namely clients, buyers, and critics, who help make a photographer's reputation, which leads to jobs.

Sales

Of course, there's also the most immediate reason to have your work shown in a gallery: *money*. Galleries are in business to make money by showing a photographer's work. They do this by assigning a dollar value to each print. Then, for every print sold, the gallery owners split the fee with the photographer, according to a financial arrangement worked out at the time the gallery agreed to exhibit the work.

So if a show attracts buyers, you not only get the ego boost of seeing your work exhibited in public, you'll make some money off sales as well.

GALLERY TYPES

There are three different types of galleries that will consider your work: privately owned, co-ops, and sponsored.

The most traditional form of exhibition is at a privately owned gallery, whose business it is to exhibit a photographer's work for the specific purpose of making sales.

Co-ops are gallery spaces where a number of photographers chip in to pay the rent and other expenses. In return for this investment, they get to use the gallery at various times to display their work.

A sponsored gallery's purpose is the exception to the rule: they do not exist to make money. Rather, because someone is sponsoring them, they can afford to show a photographer's work which might not be commercial enough to generate sales, but is good enough to produce critically favorable reviews. Those reviews reflect well not only on the photographer, but the sponsor as well. Sponsored gallery spaces can be found in places like the lobbies of large corporations and banks, the halls of ad agencies and magazines, and sometimes a separate gallery space that the sponsor rents.

Which One Should I Approach?

Since the privately owned gallery's primary reason for being is sales, they'll do all they can to reach this goal. That means publicizing the work to the public, including their clients and critics. Therefore, I suggest initially trying to get an exhibit at a privately owned gallery.

Second, I'd go with the sponsored gallery. They won't put as much effort into publicity as the private gallery, since they're not in business to make money. Instead, they want to associate the sponsor's name in the public's mind as a nurturer of talent, which, indirectly, helps publicize the sponsor's product or business. Still, this type of gallery is usually a professional operation and those who run them know how to attract an audience.

I'd look at co-ops as a third alternative. Co-ops became popular during the early 1980s, as a result of a period in the late 1970s when anyone but established photographers had difficulty getting a gallery show. Entering the late 1980s, it's a bit easier, but many photographers would rather pay a fee for a guaranteed exhibition space than go through the trauma associated with getting a gallery show in a private or sponsored gallery.

The problem is that there's a stigma attached to co-ops. It's too easy for clients and critics, the reputation makers, to say to themselves, "He wasn't good enough to get a show without paying for it." You have one strike against you when these people arrive, if they do at all. That's why I think it best to go with a co-op only if the other alternatives don't pan out.

APPROACHING THE GALLERY

Do you call, write, or show up on their doorstep with your portfolio? The best way of approaching any gallery for a show is to call them. Ask them what their policy is for viewing a photographer's work.

The larger galleries usually request that photographers drop off their work on specific days. The portfolio is kept overnight or for a few days, while a decision is made. Smaller galleries have the time to grant you a personal presentation.

Prints or Slides?

Most gallery operators prefer to see prints. It's a lot easier to take them out of the portfolio and look at them immediately than to spend the time finding a light box or slide projector.

As to type of work, once again it depends on the type of gallery. Co-ops will let you show just about anything, since you're essentially paying for the exhibit. Sponsored galleries also have a liberal policy. In contrast, privately owned galleries are forced to look for saleable work.

Now exactly what constitutes saleable work is difficult to define. It's best to do your marketing in advance; visit a couple of privately owned galleries before you make your presentation and see what's selling. This will give you a rough idea of what constitutes saleable photography at the time you make your presentation.

Financial Terms

Once the gallery agrees to exhibit your work, you have to make a financial arrangement. Generally, galleries take 50 to 60 percent of the sale and the photographer takes the rest. That means, at worst, you should be getting 40 percent. Any split where you end with less than that should not be considered.

While you need the gallery for exhibit space, they're no place without your work. Bear that in mind when negotiating, but don't be arrogant about it. Just listen to their offer and respond politely. Remember, you can negotiate at the time you agree to the show, but after the contract is signed—and you should ask for a contractual agreement—it's difficult to break it for the express purpose of getting more money. In fact, it's unprofessional.

PUTTING THE SHOW TOGETHER

After financial terms are agreed to, you have to find out what the gallery's requirements are for the exhibit. For instance, some galleries have the space for 20 × 24-inch prints or larger; some don't. You have to find out what their requirements are so you can make your prints accordingly.

If you have the money, it's always best to get someone else to do the printing for you. I know many of you won't agree with this. It's difficult to come up with a good black-and-white printer, in particular, not to mention the money to pay for the printing. There are also those photographers who believe that printing is part of the job.

Most of the photographers I know who've had gallery shows had someone else do the printing for them. The reason is, this freed them up to shoot work, on assignment, while the show was being done for them. Ask yourself the following questions:

1. Do I have the budget for printing? If not, do it yourself.

2. Can I trust someone else to do a terrific job? If not, do it yourself.

3. If I have the budget for printing, and if I trust the printer's work, should I go ahead and let him do it? Absolutely.

Framing

Galleries also have specific framing requirements. When discussing print requirements, find out about the framing requirements too. To decide whether to frame the work yourself or give it to someone who specializes in it, ask yourself the three questions above and, depending upon the answers, act accordingly.

Cocktails For Two

At gallery openings, wine and cheese are served. If the gallery is not paying for this expense (it'll be in your contract) about two weeks before the opening, arrange for the delivery of food and beverage for the night of the opening. I suggest consulting a professional caterer who specializes in this sort of party. The gallery will give you some recommendations.

Publicity

Galleries provide two types of publicity for a show. The first is the press release, sent out about three weeks before the opening. It is essential, *essential*, that the gallery send out press releases to clients and critics, in order to publicize the show and attract an audience. Without the audience, you're nowhere.

The press release should contain your brief biography and what statement you're trying to make with your photographs. The gallery usually has someone who'll ask you questions to get this information and then write it up in the form of the press release.

It's possible that you can't explain your work, that it speaks for itself. But you can't say that in a press release. You have to give people an idea of what they're going to see. Otherwise, they won't come. So when the person writing the press release asks you what you're trying to say with your work, come up with something and don't worry about how pretentious you might sound.

The second form of publicity is the invitation. This is sometimes paid for by the gallery, sometimes by the photographer, depending on the up-front agreement. The invitation goes to the same people receiving the press release. It's sent out about two weeks before the opening, and includes the gallery's phone number for an RSVP, so you'll know how many people to expect.

Most galleries will allow you to send a certain amount of invitations at their cost to clients, potential clients, and personal friends. Simply provide them with your guest list. Be aware, however, that some galleries might charge you an additional fee for this service.

Hanging The Show

A few days before the opening, the show will be hung. Depending on the gallery's policy, you can sometimes be present to offer installation suggestions. Other times, the gallery prefers letting a professional installer handle the installation of the show—alone.

The Opening

If you think taking photographs is hard, wait until you work the crowd at your opening. The opening night party can be a traumatic experience, especially if it's your first time. Clients and potential clients; critics and reporters; and family and friends will all be gathering under the same roof. You're not going to have time to have conversations with all of them, especially your personal friends, because you're not there to have a good time, but to work the crowd.

Working the crowd is a fine art. It's the ability to be polite, casual, and businesslike, all at the same time. It's greeting everyone who's been kind enough to show up, while limiting the conversation to superficialities with everyone but the reputation makers.

This is not as cynical as it sounds. There are going to be a lot of people there and you won't have time to have a conversation with everyone. You should explain this to family and friends beforehand, so they won't get offended.

The people you're trying to impress are the ones you should spend the most time with. You have to really listen to what they have to say and respond accordingly. While speaking to a client, potential client, or critic, do not tout your work. It's at this point that it has to speak for itself. That doesn't mean you should back down if your technique, subject matter, or something else about your photographs is challenged. On the contrary; you should respond in a forceful, confident manner, but without being rude. Sometimes people will be challenging your work as a test of your commitment, which is why you don't back down—ever.

If you have a conversation with someone who can do you some good, get their card. This is necessary for the follow up, which we'll discuss later. In turn, you should give them your card so they can contact you.

The best person I've ever seen at working a crowd is, strangely enough, not a photographer, but the husband of a photographer: Alan Alda.

Alda, best known as "Hawkeye Pierce" on TV's "Mash" had accompanied his wife to a New York gallery for the opening night exhibition of her photographs. Because he was there, the exhibit had attracted a lot of media attention, including TV crews. Yet Alda didn't spend any more time with the TV crews than anyone else. He walked through the crowd and talked to anyone who wanted to talk to him. He would be polite when talking about "Mash," but he made sure to turn the conversation around to the exhibit, so his wife's photography would get some publicity. It's that ability to control the conversation which Alda exhibited that typifies the most professional way of working a crowd.

When you do work the crowd, there's one thing I want to warn you about: the crashers.

Every gallery has its share of regular gate crashers. For some unknown reason, these otherworldly people manage to get their names on the mailing lists to which the press releases and invitations are sent.

When they show up, they're frequently dressed better than the "real" people. The problem arrives when they engage you in conversation. They can sound awfully intelligent and perceptive and they might very well be. But they've got no business being there and are there, in fact, fraudulently.

It's impossible to avoid them, but if you are having a conversation with someone who your intuition says is a little strange and doesn't belong, chances are he or she is a crasher. If you think this is happening, tell them you have to talk to the gallery owner about something and ask them for their card. If they're not for real, they won't have one.

Whatever you do or suspect, don't throw them out. All that will do is create an incident. Just let them enjoy the wine and cheese and forget about it.

The Follow Up

After the opening, you'll feel a big, emotional letdown. For some, such an exhibit will be the culmination of years of work. Take a couple of days off to mellow out and when you get back, you'll be fresh to begin the follow up.

The follow up can make or break an exhibit. Of course, if you've already gotten impressive reviews and client offers, the follow up isn't as important. But what happens if, and this is more likely, you haven't gotten a review yet or any job offers?

First, take care of the reviews. Ask the gallery owner for a copy of the mailing list. Review it and note the members of the press invited. Cross-check it with the sign-in book.

Every gallery has a sign-in book. It enables them to keep track of the people who attend opening night. Look at the names of the people who signed in and match them up to the journalists on the mailing list. The ones who came should be called immediately. Ask them if they liked the show and if they're going to review it. If the answer is positive, ask them when the review will run, so you can get some copies for your portfolio. If the answer is negative, don't argue. Move on to the next name.

For the press people who didn't show up, you'll have to make a "cold call." Call them up, identify yourself, and tell them about the exhibit. Ask if they would have the time to see it. If they say they'll take it in, then ask them to let you know what they think afterwards. Say something like, "I'd really appreciate your opinion."

Many photographers have trouble with this type of interpersonal communication. But people are always impressed when the artist has the courage and the confidence to do the follow up. This can lead to positive press coverage, maybe even a personal interview.

FOUR GALLERIES

To show you how galleries deal with photographers on a day-to-day basis, here are profiles of four different galleries.

THE LIGHT GALLERY

724 Fifth Avenue, New York, NY 10019

The Light Gallery is arguably the most respected private gallery in New York City. Under the watchful eye of owner Tennyson Schad, it presents exhibits that range from commercial to fine-art photography. Photographers who've been exhibited there come from a variety of cultures and countries.

"Our policy is to review a photographer's work on specific days," says Sarah Greenberg, the assistant to the gallery director. "The portfolio review takes place about twice a month," she continues.

"We'll look at any type of photography, black and white or color, prints or slides, though prints are easier to look at than slides. There are three of us here who look at the work. If we think the owner would like it, we show it to him. If the owner likes it, at that point, we consign it. Which means we take the body of work on loan from the photographer. We then include it in the roster of work we represent. Next, we send a press release to our list of clients."

The press release she's talking about should not be confused with the press release sent out in connection with an opening. This release only *goes to gallery clients.*

The reason for the limited mailing list, which does not include critics, is that not all work on consignment at the Light Gallery gets an exhibit. Instead, it may be in the gallery's viewing room, where clients can come and look and make a decision to buy or pass. Whether the photographer's work is shown in an exhibit or in the viewing room, the split is the same.

"We split 50–50, unless the work was originally commissioned by another gallery, in which case we make a different arrangement," Ms. Greenberg says.

"For shows, the gallery pays for the invitations sent out, the cocktail party—everything. That's why we think we're worth 50 percent. We also handle the follow-up calls."

As to what the gallery likes to show, Ms. Greenberg reflects, "Optimally, we'd like to show unknowns we believe in. However, that's not usually the case. We have to bring in name photographers to attract clients."

But the Light Gallery not only displays the work of individuals, they'll also mount group shows, where the work of more than one photographer is on exhibit. Meanwhile, they are always looking for new work to show.

Sarah Greenberg's best advice to photographers who want to exhibit at Light?

"It makes no difference whether a photographer dresses in jeans, a suit, whatever. What we want is someone who is cooperative, who realizes they can't come in with a portfolio and break up our day at any time, but calls ahead to find out what days we're looking at new work.

"Don't be too pushy. Try to understand our side of the business, especially when first coming in."

She reminds photographers that, at least at the beginning of a business relationship, "The ball's in our court."

SEA CLIFF PHOTO COMPANY

310 Sea Cliff Avenue, Sea Cliff, NY 11579

The Sea Cliff Photo Company is located in the artists' community of Sea Cliff, on the north shore of Long Island. It is a combination of a framing service and three gallery spaces, all under one roof, owned and operated by Don and Diann Mistretta.

"My framing operation pays the bills," says Don Mistretta. "This means I don't have to exhibit commercial work that sells all the time. I can put up something that develops a theme, like Ben Fernandez's show, 'Mental Poverty.' "

Mistretta likes to keep his options open. "The content of shows varies. I keep myself open, so I can keep up with what's happening."

"That's why, unlike other galleries, which book one year in advance, we book four to eight weeks in advance," adds Diann. She continues:

"Don reviews all the work. Just call up and make an appointment to come in. Sometimes, people come in off the street or send us slides, but we do prefer that initial call."

"When people come in with a portfolio, I may not be able to give them a show," Don says. "What I can do, though, is guide them to someone who might be more interested in their work." This points out the overall intent of the gallery, which is to be honest with the photographer.

Photographers who exhibit at the Sea Cliff Photo Company will find that the financial arrangements are quite generous. The gallery takes 40 percent of the sale, while the photographer gets 60 percent. The artist is responsible for the cost of the invitations and the opening night party, while the gallery is responsible for the press releases.

"I try to tell photographers that the most important thing about a show is the publicity. I like it when a photographer gets involved with the publicity.

"At the same time, photographers may sometimes be too overzealous in their efforts to publicize their shows. For instance, you don't go after a reviewer, corner him at the opening night party, and badger him for a good review. The reviewers will let you know in their review what they think. The last thing you want to do is provoke them.

"So it's great if the photographer helps with the initial publicity, especially getting the critics to show up. But after that, the follow up is best if it comes from a second party, namely the gallery."

Don finds that the openings take on a life of their own, depending upon the photographer whose work is on display.

"We've had anywhere from 25 to 400 people at an opening. Young guys just starting out won't get as many people (as established photographers). Then, there was a show we did of Alexander Roosevelt's photographs. The Vice Secretary of the Navy showed up as did a lot of people from Oyster Bay (a nearby, affluent community)."

Another thing Don speaks about is how he prices photographs.

"To begin with, you have to know collectors and markets. There's probably a better value, dollar for dollar, out here than in New York City, because we're more flexible and realistic.

"Specifically, I put a value on a print in two ways. First, what the market will bear. Second, the belief I have in the photographer and the photographer's belief in himself.

"If I can get $150–$175 for an 11 × 14, I'll do it. The photographer can give me his input and ask that a print be priced according to

what he wants, and I'll do it. But, I'll tell him when he's unrealistic in his demands."

Don Mistretta's advice to photographers who want to exhibit at the Sea Cliff Photo Company?

"I like dealing with a responsible, mature individual. I think the photographer's attitude and his belief in himself and his work is all-important." In contrast, nothing turns Don off more than a sloppy presentation.

As to preferences, Don says, "I prefer seeing good black-and-white prints. Sometimes, I'll get a photographer who can't print well. It doesn't matter. We can always get somebody to do that."

NIKON HOUSE

620 Fifth Avenue at Rockefeller Center, New York, NY 10020

The best example of a sponsored gallery that I can think of is Nikon House.

"The location is super," says Joe Strear. His firm, Strear, David & Mitchell, Inc., does the public relations for and helps manage Nikon House.

"Nikon House is in the middle of Rockefeller Center, right above the ice rink and across from the statue of Prometheus. It's one of New York's most heavily trafficked areas."

The gallery never has trouble attracting visitors, who get to see more than a photography exhibit.

"In addition to the gallery show displayed in the downstairs and upstairs galleries," Strear continues, "people get to see and handle the array of Nikon equipment we have in glass cases when they first walk in."

There's also a technician who sits in a small, glass-walled office, checking and repairing Nikon equipment for free. The strange thing is, despite all this product "hype," Nikon House has developed a reputation as one of the most prestigious galleries, either sponsored or private, in the city.

While the gallery was established in the 1960s, its artistic standards were developed in the late 1970s and early 1980s under the direction of its former manager, Richard Clark, Clark saw to it that only the best photographers were represented, and while there were a couple of clinkers, the place became a great showplace. Under the present management, Clark's commitment to fine photography has been continued.

"The subject matter of the exhibits is pretty unlimited," says Joe Strear. "Each month we devote the gallery to a different theme. It can be a group exhibit like A Day In The Life Of America, *or* The Annual World Press Photo Contest Award-Winning Photographs. *Other times, we'll show the work of one photographer, like Barry Peril's* Color Abstractions *or Allen Rokach's* Art In A Garden."

While the subject matter is eclectic, the procedure for getting a show is very specific. Strear comments:

"If you want a show at Nikon House, call our agency. We'll discuss our criteria with you. Then, follow up with a brief personal background, along with an explanation of what your show would consist of.

"While we respond to all queries, if we like your initial presentation, we'll arrange for your portfolio to be reviewed here at the agency."

The preferred format is 35mm. While it's impossible to tell if the shots were taken with a Nikon or not, Strear will reject any photographer who already has an association with another camera company (see next chapter).

"In any one year, we see about 500 to 600 portfolios. We narrow it down to 100, which are then sent to Nikon. The shows are then chosen by a combination of people from Nikon Professional Services and our agency. Twelve shows are selected per year. Each runs one month and we book one year in advance."

If your portfolio is chosen for exhibition, you get the added bonus of the public relations services of the agency. Strear describes this function as ". . . bringing the show to the attention of the appropriate media." What this statement boils down to is that the agency will send out press releases to the media and make follow-up calls. They will also, at their cost, send out black-and-white invitations to their media list, plus a list of clients, potential clients, and friends whose names you supply. If you want color invitations, you pay the difference between color and black-and-white ones. The agency also pays for the installation. The gallery has wall space for prints that are 11 × 14 and up.

You will have to pay for the printing and framing and the opening *night cocktail party. The latter cost is approximately $750. If you don't have a caterer in mind, Strear will recommend caterers who charge competitive prices and have done Nikon House shows in the past.*

"The opening night reception is so important," says Strear, and with good reason. It's your chance to mingle with the reputation makers. Strear and his associates will be at the opening, talking to the media and, when appropriate, introducing them to the exhibiting photographer or photographers. Photographers are also invited to leave literature explaining the show, as well as business cards.

"For young photographers, the gallery offers a good way to get public exposure," Strear reflects. "They have a good month, during the time the show is up, to get people to come down to see it.

"For the established photographer, it's also a good showplace, especially if he's doing new things, perhaps using different techniques, and wants to open a new market for his photographs."

SOHO PHOTO GALLERY

15 White Street, New York, NY 10013

According to David Chalk, the gallery director, the Soho Photo Gallery is the oldest cooperative gallery in the United States. It was formed in 1971 and is still going strong today.

"The way you become a member of the cooperative," says Chalk, "is by showing your portfolio to our members. Once a month, we look at the portfolios of prospective members. You just call for an appointment, drop the portfolio off, and you get it back the same day.

"At the time you drop it off, we ask for a $20 deposit. If you're accepted, the deposit is credited toward your membership. If you're not accepted, you get the money back. If you're accepted and choose not to join, you lose the $20." The reason for the latter response is so that photographers do not look at the gallery as a cheap portfolio evaluation service.

"We are a member-supported gallery," Chalk continues. "There are gallery dues and hanging fees. We suggest calling to find out what they currently are."

On any given month, the Soho Photo Gallery runs a number of different shows in their spacious exhibition space. There'll be a show featuring the work of a guest artist who is not a member of the co-op; four solo shows of gallery members; and in front of the gallery, there'll be mini or group shows featuring one or two works of a number of gallery members.

"There are no restrictions as to how often a co-op member can show," Chalk comments. "However, a group of members will look at a photographer's portfolio before giving him the go-ahead to hang, just to make sure the content is up-to-par. Selection of photographs displayed is left up to the photographer." There are no restrictions as to the size of prints displayed or how they are framed, but the photographer has to do his own installation because the gallery has few people on staff. As with the installation, the photographer is also responsible for doing his own pricing.

The gallery sends out invitations and press releases at no charge to the photographer. However, once again, because they have a limited staff, the photographer will frequently have to do his own follow up.

"We sometimes have a problem getting listed in The Village Voice,*" says Chalk. "They'd review the show but not list us."*

Despite this problem, the gallery exhibits a broad spectrum of photography, from photojournalism to still lifes. In fact, two of the founding members were photojournalists who worked for the New York Times.

"Some people feel co-ops are self-serving. Back when we started, though, there were few galleries displaying photographers' work and they were difficult to get into." So, in essence, the Soho Photo Gallery helped to fill that vacuum.

One added incentive to join the gallery is the workshops. "We give workshops, taught by and to members, that cost $10 or $15. We've had workshops on subjects like platinum printing and studio lighting and portraiture," says Chalk.

Photographers who've exhibited at the Soho Photo Gallery include Jill Friedman, Lee Romero, George Alpert, Zeke Berman, Joel Sternfeld, Minor White, and David Hamilton. That is quite an impressive array of talent.

SAMPLE PRESS RELEASES

To give you an idea how press releases are constructed to promote the gallery exhibit and the exhibiting photographer, here are some samples.

LIGHT

FOR IMMEDIATE RELEASE

LIGHT Gallery is pleased to announce its summer exhibition, "COMPETITION". In this wide range of fine art sports photographs created over the past 99 years, photographers have depicted the athlete interacting with the sport, the arena, the opponents and, ultimately, himself.

From Muybridge to Wegman, "COMPETITION" is a photographer's look at competitive activity. Both the reverent and cynical attitudes imposed by the photographer make these images more than mere documents. The photographic exposition of a more subtle, psychological aspect of the world of sports evokes the grace, mystery and humor of competition. The interaction of Garry Winogrand's football players, for example, is a delicately choreographed dance, while Muybridge approaches weightlifting and wrestling with a more analytical eye. Stephen Shore's Yankee Spring Training series captures the more contemplative moments of that team's preparation. Larry Fink provides the viewer with a closer look at the boxer as athlete, persona and victor. In Pittu's Olympic medallists portrait one sees the athlete as hero and monument.

LIGHT is also pleased to be highlighting Jim Dow's "SPORTS PLACES". This series of color photographs provides "COMPETITION" with a monumental, timeless context. Dow's baseball stadiums vibrate in their quiet emptiness, becoming universal symbols of the sport. They transcend the human moment and ultimately deliver their message in pure form and color.

"COMPETITION" opens Thursday, June 19th with a reception from 6-8 p.m.

FOR FURTHER INFORMATION CONTACT: Suzanne Perlstein.

724 Fifth Avenue between 56/57 New York NY 10019 212/582 6552

LIGHT

JANUARY 31 - FEBRUARY 23

PAUL BERGER

LIGHT is pleased to announce an exhibition of Paul Berger's most recent work. Mr. Berger has attempted to attach new meanings to photography and to the world around him. He has for some time been interested in the juxtaposition of visual images with narrative text. Frequently he makes his constructions out of media occurences and cultural events. By intertwining his ideas together in sequences and with multiply-exposed images Mr. Berger often creates complicated and intriguing studies of contemporary symbolism in our society.

RAY METZKER

LIGHT is pleased to announce an exhibition of Ray Metzker's Sand Creatures. This body of work recently has been published as a monograph by Aperture; Millerton, New York. In conjunction with the exhibition there will be a book signing on Februray 16th at 2-5.

The series, Sand Creatures focuses on beach life as a curious phenomenon of social intercourse. The artist has perceived with great lucidity both the diversity and territoriality of the beach inhabitants. With his ever-present formal sensibility Mr. Metzker has photographed the patterns, forms and sequences that constitute a remarkable caricature of the "sun worshiper."

724 Fifth Avenue between 56/57 New York NY 10019 212/582 6552

Nikon

NIKON HOUSE
620 FIFTH AVENUE
AT ROCKEFELLER CENTER
NEW YORK, NEW YORK 10020
(212) 586-3907

Nikon House News

STREAR, DAVID & MITCHELL, INC.
575 MADISON AVENUE
SUITE 1006
NEW YORK, NY 10022
(212) 605-0325

CONTACT: Joseph Strear

For Immediate Release

"COLOR ABSTRACTIONS" BY BARRY PERIL OPENS AT NIKON HOUSE PHOTOGRAPHY GALLERY

New York, New York, January 8, 1985 -- Color abstractions on many diverse themes form the unusual new 35 mm photography exhibition by Oregonian photographer Barry Peril which opened here today at the Nikon House Gallery in Rockefeller Center.

Mr. Peril, who runs a successful corporate and annual report photography business in Bend, Oregon, also spends time at what he calls "personal works." His spectacular color abstract photographs are examples of a "new avenue" in "personal" photography for him.

Looking at the photographs, one will marvel at the abstractions which have been created on film of such subjects as: "rust," "back-lit shrubbery," "sand and water," "rock and barnacles," "window washing," "spider web and dew," "pitcher of sun tea," "screw-detail from an old railroad car," "detail of copper frying pan," and more than 30 others.

As Peril explains: "The physical subject matter is either unknown by the viewer; or if known, of only minor importance. The

Nikon
We take the world's greatest pictures.™

photographs must work solely by means of the organization of color, texture, light and shade -- and, hopefully, with a lot of feeling too. I have chosen to work this way in order to be able to put myself into my work and to minimize the need to describe a specific time, place or thing. For me, the big reward in doing this is that, after awhile, you can find bits of yourself in everything."

Peril has previously exhibited at numerous galleries, including the Frame Design Gallery and Pinckney Center of the Arts in Bend, Oregon; Cameraworks, Lawrence, Blue Sky and Multnomah Art Center Galleries in Portland, Or.; West Com Gallery in San Francisco; and the Elliott Gallery, Croton-on-Hudson, New York, and the Museum of American Folk Art, N.Y.C., among others. He has also been featured on two "Central Oregon Today" television shows on photography, and his works have appeared in several magazines.

The free-to-the-public "Color Abstractions" by Barry Peril exhibit will be at Nikon House through Saturday, February 2. Nikon House is open Tuesday-Saturday, 10 AM-5:45 PM (closed Sunday, Monday). Nikon House is located at 620 Fifth Avenue. Its entrance is in the Channel Gardens, between 49th and 50th Sts., just west of Fifth Avenue, near the ice skating rink.

###

Nikon

Nikon House News

NIKON HOUSE
620 FIFTH AVENUE
AT ROCKEFELLER CENTER
NEW YORK, NEW YORK 10020
(212) 586-3907

STREAR, DAVID & MITCHELL, INC.
575 MADISON AVENUE
SUITE 1006
NEW YORK, NY 10022
(212) 605-0325

Contact: Joseph Strear

FOR IMMEDIATE RELEASE

"ART IN A GARDEN" EXHIBIT OPENS AT NIKON HOUSE PHOTO GALLERY, TUES., JUNE 4; PHOTOS OF FAMOUS SCULPTURES INTERACTING WITH BOTANICAL GARDEN SETTINGS

New York, New York, May 28 -- "Art In A Garden," an unusual new color photographic exhibition by prominent nature photographer Allen Rokach, showing the unique interactions between famous sculptures and their outdoor garden settings during the year's four seasons, will open at the Nikon House Gallery in Rockefeller Center on Tuesday, June 4.

This exhibit of 70 35mm dye-transfer and cibachrome prints represents a year's assignment given to Rokach by Donald Kendall, Chairman and Chief Executive Officer of PepsiCo, to document the Sculpture Gardens at PepsiCo's world headquarters in Purchase, New York.

Mr. Kendall, a man with a passion for modern art, was the driving force behind the creation of this outdoor sculpture museum. The late Russell Page, dean of garden designers, then produced a beautiful park-like setting to frame and complement each sculpture and make them accessible to the public. And, in December, 1983, Rokach was commissioned to capture on film the interaction of the sculptures and their botanical surroundings.

--more--

Nikon
We take the world's greatest pictures.™

The sculptures include "Hats Off" by Alexander Calder;"Double Oval" and "Reclining Figure" by Henry Moore; "Three People On Four Benches" by George Segal; "Eve" by Auguste Rodin;"Personnage" by Joan Miro;"Celebration II" by Louise Nevelson; and others by Max Ernst, David Wynne, Arnaldo Pomodoro, Isamu Noguchi, William Crovello, Gideon Graetz, Henri Laurens, Art Price, Asmunder Syeinson, Claes Oldenburg, and Claes Oldenburg.

Rokach took an unusual approach in his photography. With many years of experience as a nature photographer and currently the staff photographer at the New York Botanical Garden, Rokach viewed the sculptures not as fixed forms, but, rather, as living things, with distinct personalities, temperaments and moods. He knew that Russell Page thought of each sculpture as a "flower" -- the star of a particular arrangement of flowers. So, to Rokach, the constantly changing faces that they represented to him were sources of discovery. Each transformation yielded new and fascinating images. Each variation of weather presented an unexplored dimension. Each new season brought its own qualities of light and color to the sculptures and the gardens. This working concept enabled Rokach to achieve proper scale, exposure, perspective and composition in his photographs as he focused in on sculptures which looked so different from various directions.

"Many sculptors have observed that their creations are best seen out-of-doors, where viewers can witness the changing relationship

--more--

between the art and the natural surroundings. Yet, few people, even among the most ardent art lovers, actually experience such transformations," stated Rokach. "We believe that we have captured in these photographs what few of us would ever see for ourselves," he pointed out.

"Moreover, the photographs are aesthetic statements in their own right, going beyond simple documentation to a personal vision of art in a garden," he said.

Rokach has built a successful career taking pictures of the natural world he loves. In addition to being the staff photographer at the New York Botanical Garden, he is a freelance photographer whose commercial clients include many corporations and cultural institutions. His photographs have been used in advertisements, annual reports, catalogues and publicity materials, as well as in books, major international publications and photographic magazines. His prints have been exhibited at museums, nature societies and galleries throughout the metropolitan New York area, and are in several prestigious private and corporate collections.

He is also a highly-respected photographic educator, having instituted the Nature Photography Program at the New York Botanical Garden, and taught at the Camera Club of N.Y., New School for Social Research, American Museum of Natural History, Olden Photography Workshops--and recently created a specialized photography school, the Center for Nature Photography, which he directs.

--more--

"Art In A Garden" will be on exhibit at Nikon House from June 4 through June 22. It will be brought back again from Aug. 6-17 for an encore exhibit.

Nikon House is located at 620 Fifth Avenue. Its entrance is in the Channel Garden near the ice skating rink in Rockefeller Center, between 49th and 50th Streets, just west of Fifth Avenue. Its hours are: Tuesday-Saturday, from 10AM-5:45PM. It is closed Sunday and Monday.

###

CHAPTER SEVEN

Manipulating The Media

Whenever you watch TV, you are being manipulated. No matter how much you think you are immune to the pleadings of "Mr. Whipple," sooner or later you're going to break down and buy his toilet tissue, or somebody else's hair spray, dog food, or diapers.

It is the constant flow of images across the TV screen that filter into your brain, no matter how much you try to keep them out. The same thing happens with magazine ads. If you're a commercial photographer, you well understand this. You make your living creating images that convince the consumer to buy the product you're selling in your photographs.

Sometimes, you are manipulated on a much more subconscious level. Have you ever found yourself watching a TV show and seen somebody holding a product that had nothing to do with what they were talking about? I saw actress Jobeth Williams on "The Tonight Show" holding a Polaroid camera that was so new, it had barely reached the stores. I don't know how she got it, but I'll bet there were a lot of people at their local camera stores the following morning asking about that camera.

Selling goes on all the time in the media and the most basic tool for selling a product is a human being. Somebody has to be in that ad, holding that camera and saying, "This is a great camera." Somebody has to be in that commercial on TV saying, "This camera is weatherproof, earthquake-proof, everything-proof!"

Camera companies need photographers to help them promote their products. Sometimes this is done by picking out a photographer to appear in a TV or print ad. The selection is made by the camera company's public relations agency, which also does its advertising, making it a *full-service agency*, or by the camera company's advertising agency, whose only job it is to handle the company's paid marketing efforts, such as commercials and print ads.

Now TV and print ads where famous and not-so-famous photographers extol the virtues of a particular product are just one way in which the photo companies convince the public that their products are the best. Another way is to convince the *media*, and through them the public, that—you guessed it—"Our products are the best!"

This latter approach also involves promoting a product by using a photographer. In return for free equipment, a fee, or both, a photographer endorses a product. This endorsement is then printed up in *press releases*, which look like news stories, but are cleverly disguised product endorsements. These press releases are sent to photo magazines in particular, and to newspapers and general interest magazines. Frequently, they are published.

What does the camera company get out of this? After all, a press release is not a straight advertisement. The photographer mentioned in the press release is not saying "This is the best product since creation." What he's probably saying is something like, "On my way up K2 in Nepal, I used my name-brand camera to take pictures of my Sherpa guide as he . . ." Notice, however, that the product got mentioned. Let's go back to the TV commercial with "Mr. Whipple." Sooner or later, you're going to buy the product he endorses, because, on a subliminal level, your mind remembers its name when you go in the supermarket and you reach for Whipple's toilet paper.

The same thing happens when a consumer goes in to buy a camera. He remembers seeing the name of the camera in that "article" about the photographer climbing K2. Guess which camera he asks for?

This is the way the media manipulates the consumer into buying a particular product, regardless of the product's relative merit. There is nothing you can do to stop this. In fact, it's what the United States is built on: the free enterprise system.

What you can do is to turn it around. You can manipulate the media for your own gains, because somebody—some photographer—is helping sell those products and it might as well be you. That's right, you. Turn around and look in the mirror. See that guy there? He's about to enter the wonderful world of public relations.

THE GOAL

The goal of the promotion we will be talking about is to get a camera company to promote you and your work, in return for your helping to promote their products. They will pay you to do this in the following ways: free publicity (the press releases), free equipment, a fee, a gallery exhibit of your photographs, or any combination of these elements. In addition, you may be asked to appear on TV talk shows. You can cope with that, can't you? You'll be talking about the unique work you do, and in the course of the interview, you'll just happen to mention the name of the camera you use. Don't think that you have to be doing something as dramatic as scaling K2 to get a camera company to promote you. Let's take the case of Jacques Kaplan.

Jacques Kaplan was a retired furrier who had a heart attack. As part of his recovery, his doctor recommended walking. After doing that for awhile, Jacques got bored.

On his next walk, Jacques brought along his camera, a Canon. He began taking abstract photographs, making things like garbage look graphically stunning. Eventually, Canon found out about his endeavors and got him on "The Today Show," where he talked about his work. During the course of the interview, the name Canon was mentioned.

Kaplan was not paid a fee to help promote Canon cameras. Instead, he received incalculable amounts of free publicity. I know—I wrote two articles about him. One was a layout for the Sunday magazine of the New York *Daily News*, the other a profile for *The Rangefinder*.

Jacques Kaplan is now a working photographer. He does quite well exhibiting and selling his photographs in galleries. In Kaplan's case, the camera company came to him. Most of us aren't that lucky. We have to go to them.

THE AGENCY

Most camera companies, known as the client, employ a public relations agency. The client pays the agency a set fee, plus billable expenses, to publicize their products in the broadest possible manner. They attempt to achieve this goal in the following ways.

Press Releases

The agency regularly writes and distributes press releases. The bulk of them extol the virtues of the client's products with an excessive amount of adjectives and adverbs. Known in the trade as product publicity, these are published sometimes verbatim, in some trade and consumer photography magazines.

Press Conferences

We've already mentioned them. Usually held in some large, prestigious hotel in New York City like the Plaza, journalists both in and out of the photography business are invited to see the product, have a hands-on demonstration, and then take home the press kit.

Press Kits

Press kits are another kind of product publicity. They contain all kinds of technical information about the new camera and its accessories. Photographs of the products are also provided. Press releases that were previously issued about older products might also be included.

Promotions

This is where you come in. As mentioned earlier, the agency will use photographers to help promote their client's products. Press releases about you and your work, TV appearances, and gallery exhibits are the forms of promotion involving photographers.

THE AGENCY/CLIENT RELATIONSHIP

Despite the agency's best efforts, the client is rarely, if ever, satisfied. The client always wants more for his money. This means the agency is always on edge, because at any moment, the client may take his business elsewhere.

Because the agency is aware that they constantly have to come up with new ideas to please their client, they are amenable to listening to proposals from photographers that can help them publicize the client's products.

Amenable does not mean easy acceptance. Public relations people immediately ask, "What's in it for us?" This is the bottom line. If you can convince them that your proposal will help publicize the product, you've got 'em.

Before moving on, let me offer a warning. Public relations people are on duty 24 hours a day. They literally sell their souls on the altar of their client's logo, for which they receive high salaries. They will nail you within an inch of your life if it benefits their client.

Whatever agreement you make with the agency, *get it in writing.* Then get a lawyer to look it over and make sure it's binding between both parties.

THE HOOK

Now that you understand the benefits of agency promotion, as well as the caution you should exercise, begin to think about what you have to promote.

First, look at your personal background. Did you get into photography in an unusual way, like Jacques Kaplan? Have you had to triumph over some sort of physical adversity to succeed? Has your family been in photography for one generation or more?

What I'm asking is: what makes you unique? That uniqueness of character is something that can be used to promote yourself. It is the "hook" that will get the agency interested enough to want to promote you.

Another hook is something unusual about your work. I know one photographer who did a series of portraits of people who appeared in Times Square peep shows. She used those portraits, which were not in any way obscene, to promote herself and her photography. Now, this is certainly unusual, but that's the point: the more unusual the elements in your work, the more you have to promote.

Here are some sample promotional hooks, divided up according to photographic specialties.

1. Wedding Photography: You shot the wedding of some sort of celebrity, an actor, politician, or sports star.

2. Portrait Photography: You photographed the heads of a number of major corporations.

3. School Photography: You've been in the same town for 30 years and have photographed three generations of the same families.

4. Architectural Photography: You photographed the most famous buildings in your town, some of which, despite their elegance, have fallen to the wrecker's ball.

5. Photojournalism: In the course of your work, you've photographed major news stories.

6. Fashion Photography: Every year you photograph the line of clothes for a prominent designer. Maybe your photographs include those of a well-known model.

7. Commercial Photography: You've found ingenious photographic solutions to your client's problems. Your photographs subsequently helped sell the product in magazine ads.

In all these cases, you've kept the rights to your photographs. They can be shown to the public, whether disseminated to magazines and newspapers with a press release, on TV during an interview, or in a gallery exhibit. The photographs are promoting *you*, and if you use your imagination, you'll find a lot of hooks within your work that make it special.

Project Support

Another type of hook is an interesting project you either are working on presently or contemplating working on in the near future.

When I worked for the agency that represented Nikon, I was approached by people every day who were interested in having Nikon promote them on the basis of some undertaking.

There was the photographer taking a walking tour of the United States; the couple who were setting off on an expedition to find a lost tribe in the South Pacific; the photographer who wanted to shoot an all-women's mountaineering team as they scaled Devil's Tower in Wyoming; the scientific institute that was going to locate and photograph the Titantic (they missed out because of bad weather); and many, many others.

What most of these people wanted was equipment and their stories in press releases. Some also wanted financial support, which amounted to endorsement fees, for their projects. In return for the money, they agreed to mention the product in press releases, on TV talk shows, and also in magazine ads.

Who did the agency promote? The ones who had a valid idea to begin with, ideas that were interesting and exciting, and most importantly, the ones who presented their ideas in a coherent manner.

THE PITCH

Presentation; it separates the pros from the amateurs. How can you make a presentation to the agency that's guaranteed to attract their attention?

You've already begun by deciding what your hook is going to be. Next, you have to write it up. For this, you'll need your letterhead stationery, a typewriter or word processor with good letter quality, and enough time to polish the query so that it reads in easy-to-understand English.

The query or proposal should not run longer than 400 to 500 words, double-spaced, on a single sheet. Margins should be set up so the copy is easy to read.

The query should begin with a "grabber," a sentence that grabs the reader and makes him want to go further. Then, proceed to outline in the first paragraph why your hook is so important, but don't overstate the case. Simply tell the agency why you think their interests dovetail with yours.

In succeeding paragraphs, outline the proposal further. End with the request for what you want from the agency. I suggest you start by asking for equipment and press-release promotion. You can discuss fees later, once you're in the office.

If you can afford it, get a professional writer to go over your query and correct it for grammar and spelling. Once that's done, send it out to the agency. The person you will be sending it to is the account supervisor (see separate list). Make sure you send it with a return receipt requested. This will tell the account supervisor that you think enough of the proposal to want it handled by him personally.

ARRANGING A MEETING

This is the part where you're going to have to be patient. Agencies receive queries all the time and they usually take a while, up to two months, to respond.

What I suggest doing is waiting one month and then calling the account supervisor to confirm that he received the proposal. By this time, of course, you have the return receipt in hand, and you know he's received it. But now you're jogging his memory and forcing a response.

If you've prepared your proposal professionally, and if you continue to follow up with polite phone calls, eventually you will get a meeting with the agency.

THE MEETING

The meeting will usually be conducted by the account supervisor. He cannot give a yes or no answer to the proposal. What he can do is discuss it, and make recommendations to his client.

A warning, again. If your meeting is set up with the account executive rather than the account supervisor, ask that the account supervisor also be present. The AE is pretty far down the totem pole. He first has to report to the account supervisor before anything is sent to the client for their approval. Therefore, bear in mind when you're dealing with the agency that you're dealing with a *bureaucracy*. It is to your benefit to have a person with a certain amount of clout, like the account supervisor, in on the meeting.

At the meeting, you will make a verbal pitch for the agency to promote you. You will reiterate what the hook is. Three reactions are possible:

1. They may be completely turned off, in which case it's time to take your business elsewhere.

2. They may like the hook.

3. They may come up with another hook, something you hadn't even thought about.

If the result is points two or three, the next thing they will want to discuss is the deal: what they will do for you and what you will do for them.

NEGOTIATING THE DEAL

Now is the time to be confident and forceful, to act like what you are: a respected, professional photographer, willing to lend your time and effort to the promotion. What will the agency offer in return?

Agencies usually begin by offering free equipment, for which the photographer agrees to allow himself to be publicized in press releases in the manner previously discussed.

When the press release is sent out, they might want to include one of your photographs. Also, ask if you can include a head shot of yourself. This will give you a separate identity from your competitors.

If you're going to be shooting something unusual, the agency will want the use of those photographs to accompany the press release. The photographs could also be used to form a gallery show, which the agency sponsors (see previous chapter).

In some instances, the photographer will also be paid money in return for his cooperation with the agency promotion. TV "spots" or appearances might also be part of this package.

When can a photographer negotiate a fee? When he is either a big name, has a "scoop" on unusual photographs (like the discovery of the Titanic), or the photographs he is about to take are bound to be newsworthy, like pictures of a famous sporting event like the America's Cup.

If you think that your promotion should involve a fee, and the agency is willing to discuss it, do not attempt to negotiate it yourself. Get a photographer's representative or some other sort of agent to do the negotiating for you. This is a much more professional way of doing business. Also, you may not be aware of the market value for the type of promotion in question, while a rep or an agent would.

As I cautioned earlier, whatever agreement you reach, make sure it's reviewed by your lawyer and contracts are signed between you and the agency, so each knows the responsibility of the other in the deal just negotiated.

The following is a list of agencies who represent major camera companies. They are the ones who should be approached with your initial query and *not* their client. The client is paying the agency to screen such proposals and if you attempt to bypass the agency and go directly to the client, it won't do you any good; they'll just kick it back to the agency for evaluation anyway.

AGENCY CONTACTS

In these listings, you'll find the name of the position that handles proposals from photographers. I've stayed away from specific names because the world of public relations is volatile and people change jobs frequently. When you contact the agency, find out the name of the person who is currently in the position indicated.

Also note that clients sometimes change their agencies. If you find, after consulting the listings, that the client is no longer using the agency indicated, and the old agency refuses to give you the name of the new agency handling the account, contact the client directly. They'll be glad to supply you with the information.

THE ROWLAND COMPANY
415 Madison Avenue
New York, NY 10017
(212) 688-1200

The Rowland Company represents Canon. Contact the account supervisor.

DANIEL J. EDELMAN, INC.
1775 Broadway
New York, NY 10019
(212) 757-9100

Daniel J. Edelman, Inc., represents Fuji. Contact the account supervisor.

BOZELL AND JACOBS, KENYON AND ECKHARDT
6 East 43 Street
New York, NY 10017
(212) 916-8500

Bozell and Jacobs, Kenyon and Eckhardt, represents Minolta. Contact the agency vice-president in charge of the Minolta account.

STREAR, DAVID & MITCHELL, INC.
575 Madison Avenue
Suite 1006
New York, NY 10022
(212) 605-0325

Strear, David & Mitchell, Inc. represents Nikon. Contact the agency president.

OLYMPUS
Crossways Park
Woodbury, NY 11797
(516) 364-3000

Olympus is the only one of the major camera companies to have their own, in-house public relations operation. Contact the press representative.

E. B. WILSON PUBLIC RELATIONS
136 Madison Avenue
New York, NY 10016
(212) 213-0200

E. B. Wilson Public Relations represents Ricoh. Contact the account supervisor.

MANHATTAN COMMUNICATIONS
1142 Manhattan Avenue
Suite CP 262,
Manhattan Beach, CA 90266
(213) 546-1666

Manhattan Communications represents Vivitar. Contact general partner Ron Leach.

A FALLBACK POSITION

If you strike out with the agencies, you can still promote yourself in the electronic media, through TV and radio appearances.

Like agency promotions, you'll need a hook and pitch letter. I suggest taking a look at the query you originally submitted to the agencies. See if you got some good, constructive criticism on why it didn't work. If you did, rewrite it, repairing the faulty parts. If not, and you're satisfied with the pitch despite the rejections, simply type it up again and submit it to the new markets—by return receipt, of course. Apply the same follow-up procedures that were used with the agencies.

RADIO PROMOTION

Every city has a radio station and every station has at least one discussion show a week, on which you can make an appearance.

Because radio is a verbal medium, you'll be confined to talking about your photographs. So a radio appearance should be designed to promote yourself as a photography expert, making sure to mention what kind of photography you do and where you can be contacted. This can be a very effective way of drumming up new business.

Radio is also a good place to promote a gallery exhibit, but timing is everything. If you want a lot of people at the opening, try to go on the radio show the day before. If you want to build crowds, go on while the exhibit is running.

In terms of the actual appearance, make some notes before you show up at the studio, which you can refer to while being interviewed. Remember, it's radio, and no one will see them. Speak into the microphone in a clear voice. Don't try to sound like Walter Cronkite. It won't work. Just talk like you always do and you'll be fine.

You can buy a great source of radio shows called *Radio Contacts*. It's published by Larimi Communications Associates, Ltd., 151 East 50 Street, New York NY 10022. *Radio Contacts* is revised every year, so it's always up-to-date. It lists the names, addresses, telephone numbers, and staff of all the major radio stations in the United States. Included are complete descriptions of local, syndicated, and network discussion shows, including what each show looks for in the way of guests.

TELEVISION PROMOTION

Let me tell you what a TV promotion *can't* do. I had been booked to appear on "The Joe Franklin Show," to promote a book I had written. I went on the show, hyped the book and felt great—until I found out that my publisher had let me go on *before* the book had been shipped to bookstores. While no one can measure the effect of a TV appearance on sales, one thing was certain: from a business point-of-view, I wasted my time. Personally, I had a blast.

The moral of the story is that TV is an imperative medium. The images are fleeting and don't stay on people's minds. That's why your appearance should be geared toward promoting something that is happening or about to happen immediately, whether it's a new ad campaign breaking that features your photographs, or the opening of a gallery exhibit.

Yet, despite the incredible power of the televised image, which penetrates millions of homes, most photographers would never think of promoting themselves and their work on television. Indeed, most of us think of TV appearances as off-limits to anyone except celebrities, politicians and Charo.

Of course, this just isn't true. Many times, photographers appear on TV talk shows to discuss and show their work. For instance, a photographer who was documenting the schedule of the great philanthropist Dr. Armand Hammer was a guest on "The Tonight Show." While talking to Johnny Carson about his work, he also showed some of his photographs.

Walter Iooss, Jr. was on many TV talk shows, including "The Merv Griffin Show," to discuss his role in creating a photodocumentary of the 1984 Olympics for the Fuji Film Company. There have also been TV specials in prime time about photographers and their work. Pete Turner, a commercial photographer, even had his own photography program on a cable TV station.

I should also mention that the standard TV talk shows will not be the only market for an appearance. Occasionally, TV broadcasts shows devoted exclusively to photography, like the aforementioned Pete Turner's "The Photographer's Eye" and the syndicated "World of Photography."

Check *TV Contacts* for any photography shows currently airing. Also, check your local edition of *TV Guide*. If you see a photography show listed that isn't included in *TV Contacts*, watch the show—

which you should do in any case—and get the name of the production company and where it's located, which is usually listed in the credits. Then contact the production company directly about going on the photography show that they produce.

One other market for TV appearances is your local cable TV stations, including the public access channels. Because they have so much time to fill, local cable stations are always looking for guests. They, too, should be contacted.

Wedding and portrait photographers in particular should take note of this market. It's an ideal way to promote yourself, without spending a penny, in your local community. An appearance on the local cable TV station might also spur a reporter to do an article about you and your business in the local newspaper, which would provide even more free publicity.

Bookings

Booking yourself on a TV show takes a lot of phone calls and hard work, but it can be done. If you stick with it, you'll be successful. Why am I so sure? Because TV is a voracious medium, constantly eating up "product," and anything that appears on the tube, including human beings, is "product."

If you buy a copy of *TV Contacts*, which, like its sister volume, is published by Larimi Communications (same address), you'll have a resource that contains listings of TV talk shows around the country, including the people at each show in charge of booking guests. Once you pick out the city you want to concentrate on, contact all the TV talk shows within that geographic area. Once again, go back to your pitch letter and the by now standard follow-up procedures.

Speaking of follow up, you'll probably have to make a lot of follow-up calls to the contact at the TV program to make sure he received your proposal. Then you'll have to convince him you're a viable guest on the show he handles. Like before, you should have a pleasant, but forceful, phone manner.

The Appearance

When you eventually break through and book your first appearance, which you will, the next step is to dress for television.

Stereotypically, photographers have been portrayed in movies and TV as sloppy, ill-kept people. You're going to have to fight that stereotype and a primary way to do so is in the way you dress. Don't wear any loud colors or patterns. Dress in a conservative suit or sports jacket and slacks, dress shirt and tie. Women should wear a dress or business suit. You want to project a business-like image, which the viewer will find attractive.

Make sure you get to the studio well in advance of the taping or live broadcast, whichever it may be. You'll be asked to sign a waiver, something to the effect that you won't sue the station if a light falls down on your head and kills you. Sign it. No one's been killed by a falling light in television for years—I think.

Next, you'll be ushered into the make-up room, where a make-up artist will apply the orange powder that gives skin a healthy appearance under the hot TV lights. On some shows, there is no make-up artist. In that case, apply the make-up yourself, giving your face a light dusting, just to take the sheen off.

With the exception of "The Tonight Show," where a boom microphone is used, TV talk shows employ lavalier mikes, which attach to the front of your shirt like a tie pin. Because there's a wire sticking out of it, your range of movement is restricted, so don't stand up suddenly. Otherwise, the sound man will have a fit.

Take a couple of deep breaths before the show goes on and collect your thoughts. Listen to the questions the host asks you and answer truthfully. Don't gesticulate. Keep your hands in your lap. Any excess movement appears wild and unassociated on camera.

There'll be one camera on you when you speak. You can tell which one it is by the red light that goes on to indicate it's in use. Don't look at this camera, however. Just be aware of which one it is, because you'll naturally play to it.

Make sure that you tape your TV appearance on a VCR. The tape can then be used as a separate promotional tool, to show prospective clients in your studio who may not have seen it before.

Speaking Engagements

Top off your free promotional efforts by soliciting speaking engagements. At trade photography shows there are seminars, where photographers lecture photographers on a variety of topics, from business to aesthetic subject matter. There is a lot of prestige associated with speaking to your peers as an expert and something else: money.

CHAPTER EIGHT

Developing a Free Promotion Campaign

Now that you understand what free promotion is all about, think about establishing a free, promotional program of your own. For your consideration, here are a number of different programs that utilize free promotional elements. They are broken down according to photographic specialty.

WEDDING AND PORTRAIT

Let's begin with the toughest specialty to promote: wedding and portrait work.

I say the toughest because the wedding and portrait photographer is taken for granted. He is not accorded the respect due his profession because what he does looks so easy. With the proliferation of compact 35mm cameras, is a common belief that anyone can snap a shot at a wedding.

This is wrong, of course, but the wedding photographer has to consider people's misconceptions when promoting himself. However, when that same photographer goes into the studio to shoot portraits, he has it a little easier. He can have a lighting set-up that makes him look like a pro, but that's still not enough to change people's minds. How then can the wedding and portrait photographer overcome these negative preconceptions, at least to some extent, and use the elements of free promotion to further his business?

Editorial

The Rangefinder, *The Professional Photographer*, and *Studio Photography* publish numerous profiles of wedding and portrait specialists. If you contact the magazines directly, or one of their writers, you eventually will get a profile in one of them, including pictures.

After the article is published, laminate it and display it on the walls of your studio's reception area, where prospective clients can see it as soon as they walk in. Believe me, it'll impress them.

Copies can also be Xeroxed and sent out as a mailing to old clients, who might recommend you to friends, relatives, or neighbors, and to prospective clients who might have need of your services.

Speaking Engagements

The Professional Photographers of America trade shows, including the state conventions and the national one, have seminars where wedding photographers share the secrets of their success with their brethren. As stated earlier, the seminar speakers generally get paid a fee for their appearance, plus expenses.

To speak at these conventions, contact the organizers of the show you're interested in. Lists of upcoming shows appear every month in *The Rangefinder*.

To teach a seminar, send the organizers a written proposal of what you plan to discuss. There are so many of these conventions held every year and qualified speakers are always in demand. Eventually, you will break through, but don't stop after the first seminar. Keep teaching at these trade shows, until the rank and file begin to know who you are and acknowledge you as an expert in the field.

Camera Company Promotions

After your credentials are established, contact the manufacturers of the medium-format equipment used by wedding photographers. Direct a proposal to them to help promote their products.

TV Appearances

Next up, book yourself on a TV talk show as a wedding expert. Who better to advise brides and grooms how to look good on camera at a wedding than you? Who better to advise brides and grooms what to look for when they go out to buy a wedding photography package? You could also bring models along with you to the studio. On camera, use the models to show the bride and groom how to pose when being photographed.

Gallery Exhibits

I think there's limited potential for a gallery exhibit of your wedding photographs. The public just doesn't find them interesting enough to purchase. However, if your portraits are well executed, you could contact some local galleries about getting an exhibit of them.

There's one other point I'd like to make about wedding and portrait photographers before moving on. At least 75 percent of the ones I've known over the years have wanted to move into commercial photography. This is an extremely difficult task, because of the preconceptions I mentioned earlier. However, I believe this can be done, but only through promoting yourself as a photography expert.

Whether you're doing a magazine interview or a TV talk show, make sure you mention that you do other types of photography. All you need is that one client who comes to you to shoot a commercial job, and you've begun building your commercial portfolio. If you then add self-assigned commercial shots to the ones you've already created on assignment, you should have a good enough portfolio to promote yourself as a commercial photographer. Eventually, you could be leaving the wedding field forever.

COMMERCIAL

Commercial photographers are essentially promotional experts. The key to their success is their ability to promote a product with their photographs. They also have the advantage of laboring under a "carry along" philosophy. That is, if they promote themselves correctly, they can be identified as the photographer who shoots the ads for a name brand of soft drink, perfume, or other product. This identity as a name brand shooter reflects back on the photographer and provides him with an audience who has already seen and respects his work.

Endorsements

I'd go for the jackpot first. Nothing beats getting paid to endorse a product. I touched on endorsements in Chapter Seven, but let me go into a little more detail now.

If you read photography magazines, you've seen endorsements. The ads may show a photographer's work, usually some striking color shot, and then near it is some copy that reads: "John Smith, famous commercial photographer, used a Brand X camera to take these shots." Then, there's a quote from John, something to the effect of, "I could only take these wonderful shots because the equipment I chose was Brand X." There's also a variation on this type of ad, that includes a head shot of John, but whether his picture is in the ad or not, he's going to be quoted.

Do the photographers really use the equipment? Obviously, the camera companies say they do, but there's no way to be sure.

I also remember being in an ad agency executive's office, as he was paging through *American Photography Showcase*, looking for a photographer to endorse his client's camera equipment. He told me that the guy didn't have to use the equipment, he just had to have some great shots to use in ads. That's the business you'll be getting into if you go for endorsements.

How do you promote yourself to the agencies who produce endorsement ads? Remember, they're always looking, so they are willing to listen. "They" in this case is *not* the public relations agency, but the *advertising agency*. The PR agency will tell you who their client's ad agency is. You should contact the person in charge of that account at the ad agency with a letter from you offering your services.

The letter should emphasize your association with name clients and your interest in promoting the company's equipment. Offer to stop by and show them your portfolio. If you get called in, just have a preliminary discussion. Don't attempt to do the negotiating yourself. Get a rep or a lawyer to do this for you.

As I said at the beginning of this section, endorsements can be a jackpot, but they're a crapshoot. Most of the time, the agency will go directly to the photographer with whose work they're familiar. Still, take a shot at contacting them. If you can get in the door, you may not get an endorsement contract, but they may give you an assignment to shoot an ad for the camera company and that's not bad either.

Camera-Company Promotion

If you've tried and failed to get an endorsement deal from the ad agency, contact the camera company's public relations agency with a promotional idea. Be sure it's carefully thought out. You want to convince them the first time out that their interests coincide with yours. Ask for equipment to shoot a special project you're working on. In return, agree to let them use your photos in press releases advertising the promotion.

Editorial

Commercial photographers command more respect from editors and writers than wedding and portrait photographers, perhaps because journalists look at the commercial shooter as working in a more competitive marketplace. Whatever the reason, it's a lot easier for a commercial photographer to get an article in a consumer photography magazine.

I said easier, not easy. You're still going to have to convince the magazine that you are unique enough to merit a profile or layout.

I'd start my editorial assault on the consumer magazines as follows: *American Photographer*, *Popular Photography*, *Modern Photography*, *Photographer's Forum*, *Petersen's Photographic*, and *Photo District News*.

If you strike out with all of these, hit the trade magazines in this order: *Photo/Design*, *The Rangefinder*, and if you get absolutely desperate, *Studio Photography*.

Gallery Exhibit

Many galleries, like the Light Gallery and Nikon House, exhibit the work of commercial photographers. Use the *Yellow Pages* to make a list of the galleries in your area, then call them to find out which ones are interested in your work.

TV Appearances

A TV appearance can be used to promote an upcoming gallery exhibit, or to promote yourself as a photography expert. For instance, you can suggest to the guest coordinator of the TV show that you come on right before Thanksgiving, Christmas, or New Year's. You can offer suggestions for photographing family gatherings and parties, as well as discussing the different types of cameras that can be used. Be sure to bring along some of your photographs as illustrations.

Speaking Appearances

Like wedding photographers, commercial photographers can benefit from speaking appearances too.

Trade shows are one place to speak. In recent years, it's become popular to speak at Photo Expo, a trade show for professional photographers, run by Conference Management Company and sponsored by *Photo District News*, which is once a year on both the east and west coasts. The literature that is sent to photographers who are thinking of attending; to camera, equipment, and film manufacturers who rent booths at the shows; and to the media covering the shows, indicate which photographers are teaching what seminars. Head shots are included, so the photographer is not just a name on paper.

The commercial photographer gets a lot of exposure to the photo industry at large by teaching a seminar at a trade show like Photo Expo, or one of the regional or the national PPA shows, for that matter. Photo companies looking for photographers to do endorsements will take special interest in seminar speakers, whose prestige and influence within the photo community is reflected in the fact that they were asked to appear. The assumption is that people will listen to what they have to say.

The photographer will also get a fee for speaking at the show. In addition, a speaking engagement gives the photographer an opportunity to promote other projects he's working on, such as a book of his photography or a videotape.

Commercial photographers should also think about teaching at a photo workshop, such as the well-known Maine Photographic Workshop held each summer.

Teaching in these situations carries with it an inordinate amount of attention, because all the photo media carry some sort of article about who's teaching what and where. These articles are generally published in the spring, so photographers have time to enroll in the workshops.

Teaching at a photo workshop not only gets you publicity through the photo media, it also gets you a fee for your services. If you want to teach at a workshop, the time to send out your queries is in the fall, when the schools are getting their faculty ready for the coming semester. To get a list of the photo workshops, phone *Popular Photography*, *Modern Photography*, *The Rangefinder*, or any other photo publication you regularly read or subscribe to. Ask for one of the senior editors and tell him you'd like to know in which back issue they published their list of the photo workshops. If you subscribe to that magazine, you might have that back issue in your house, garage, or studio. If not, the library might have it. If all else fails, ask the editor if you can purchase the back copy. Rarely will they say no.

Once you have the list, you'll notice that workshops are held all over the country, in places as diverse as Maine and New Mexico. It might be more convenient to approach a workshop in your geographic area, especially if the workshop will only pay a fee for your services and no expenses.

Once you've decided which workshops to approach, contact the director of each particular workshop by phone. If he sounds interested, follow up with a letter and your portfolio, if requested, and keep following up until you get a definite yes or no. Remember: any agreement should be confirmed in writing.

PHOTOJOURNALISM

Photojournalists cover everything from celebrities to wars and there's a wealth of promotional opportunity within this photographic specialty.

Camera Company Promotion

Begin by approaching a camera company and describing an upcoming assignment. If it has anything to do with the news—covering a war, political unrest in the U.S. or abroad, or an unusual achievement in sports, like the Olympics—I think you have a good chance. If you've had similar assignments in the past, and can show a portfolio that proves this, it establishes your reputation and the camera company will have a hard time turning you down.

They'll supply you with equipment and probably want to use your photographs in press releases, which is all right, provided they've already been sold elsewhere. You should also discuss the possibility of an exhibit of the photographs being taken with their equipment. This provides the camera company—and you—with an additional promotional opportunity.

Editorial

The work of photojournalists lends itself to profiles and layouts in consumer magazines. Contact them in this order: *American Photographer*, *Popular Photography*, and *Petersen's Photographic*.

TV Appearances

As a photojournalist, you can speak about the things that you've photographed. Without knowing it, you may be considered an expert on something that you've covered in depth, and TV shows like nothing more than putting on experts.

Let's say you covered a war in a South American country and have terrific pictures. Call up the TV show, telling them who you are and what you do, and say that you want to discuss your experiences. Of course, the smaller the city, the better your chance of appearing on the show, because there's less competition. In larger cities, the TV show guest coordinator also has the ability to attract acknowledged political experts. Still, nothing beats listening to someone who's been someplace that's in the headlines, and has the pictures to prove it.

Pictures of the Year

The true purpose of photojournalism can sometimes be overshadowed by somewhat unscrupulous photographers who use photographs to exploit rather than shed light on human emotions.

There are many more photographers working today, though, who adhere to a sense of ethical responsibility. It's to honor the photojournalists with a conscience that the University of Missouri conducts its Picture of the Year (POY) competition.

POY is sponsored by the National Press Photographers Association (NPPA) and the University of Missouri School of Journalism, under an educational grant from one of the camera companies. As of publication, it was Canon.

In the newspaper division, "bests" are awarded in the following categories: spot news, general news, feature picture, sports action, sports feature, portrait/personality, pictorial, editorial illustration, fashion illustration, food illustration, news picture story, feature picture story, sports picture story, self-produced published picture story—broadsheet, and self-produced published picture story—multi-page, tabloid.

In the magazine division, winners are divided into the following categories: news/documentary, feature, sports, portrait/personality, pictorial, science/natural history, published picture story, and self-edited picture story.

In addition, there is an overall winner in each category, plus a separate photo-essayist category.

Winning in one of the top three categories at POY—Magazine Photographer of the Year, Newspaper Photographer of the Year, or Photo Essay Award of the Year—all entail concomitant publicity. Specifically, the camera company sponsoring the contest arranges interviews for you in photo magazines and, sometimes, on TV; your work will be included in a traveling exhibit of POY winners; and you also win camera equipment and a cash award.

For more information about this contest, contact: Pictures of the Year Director, University of Missouri School of Journalism, Columbia, Missouri.

Gallery Exhibits

Many galleries exhibit the work of photojournalists. Galleries are a good place to have your work seen by a larger group of people than just the ones who read the magazine or newspaper for which you photograph.

FASHION PHOTOGRAPHERS

Fashion photographers are perceived by those in and outside of the photo industry as working in some Valhalla of glamour. Never mind that it's a lot of hard work making some model who's been up late the night before look beautiful.

Yet regardless of the reality, fashion photography has such a glamorous reputation that the fashion photographer can use this misperception to his advantage.

TV Appearances

More than any other type of photography, the fashion photographer uses sex to sell a product, whether it be the dress the model is wearing or the perfume bottle she's holding in her carefully manicured hands. So the promotional element of any TV appearance should entail a certain amount of sex.

Propose to the guest coordinator of the TV talk show in your area that you simulate a fashion photography session on the air, from start to finish. This would include having a stylist and make-up person with you, plus the model, but you could probably get them to do it for nothing provided you mention their name on the air.

During the session, the audience can watch as the model is made up, dressed up, and taken to the set. They can watch as you pose and then photograph them.

It is during the actual, simulated shoot that you will show the audience what your craft is all about. In one sense, you'll be demystifying fashion photography. Don't worry, though, the audience is still going to think you're in a glamorous profession when they take one look at the model in full make-up and wardrobe.

From a business point of view, a TV appearance like the one described will establish you in the audience's mind as an expert fashion photographer. Potential clients may see the broadcast and offer you jobs. A gallery might contact you for an exhibit of your work. The point is, what good is it remaining anonymous in your studio? You have to get out there and let people know who you are.

Endorsements

Getting back to perceptions, I think fashion photographers are viewed by clients and public alike, as being more akin to artists than commercial photographers. And since the camera-buying public tend to be hard-working individuals, it is the more "nuts-and-bolts" commercial shooters who are used in endorsements to sell equipment. It is not surprising, then, that these commercial photographers generally tend to get the bulk of the endorsements.

This doesn't mean that a fashion photographer shouldn't try for an endorsement. But since promotional time is limited, you may be better able to put that time to work in other areas.

Camera Company Promotion

If you fail at getting an endorsement, try to get a camera company promotion deal. Again, because so much of what a fashion photographer does is tied up with beauty and glamour, these elements are the ones to emphasize when approaching the camera company's public relations agency.

Gallery Exhibits

The opening night part of a fashion photographer's gallery exhibit can be more important than the opening night party for a photographer working in one of the other specialties because fashion photographers have the best possibility of "breaking through."

"Breaking through" is when a photographer's name and reputation transcend his profession. He becomes a name with whom the general public is familiar. We are talking about fame and it can begin at the opening night party.

The opening night parties for fashion photographers generally attract large crowds that are frequently composed of celebrities, politicians, any of those people you're always reading about in *People* magazine.

You might see an item in the gossip columns stating that Liza Minnelli attended the opening of fashion photographer John Smith's photographs at the Light Gallery. That's how it happens. The fashion photographer attracts celebrities, and if the person promoting the exhibit is smart, he'll use those celebrities to help promote the exhibiting photographer.

Editorial

Once again, consumer magazines should be contacted first, in this order: *American Photographer*, *Popular Photography*, *Modern Photography*, *Petersen's Photographic*, and *Photographer's Forum*. In the trade magazine area, try *Photo/Design* and *The Rangefinder*.

CORPORATE AND ANNUAL REPORT

Most of the public doesn't know what a corporate and annual report photographer does. He may be well-known to the companies that employ him, but to the public, he's an unknown quantity. The key to his promotion program is going to be education.

TV Appearances

The guest coordinator will probably think that what you do sounds boring. "So you take pictures in factories," might be a typical comment. After this initial cynicism, ask the guest coordinator to take a look at your portfolio.

Some of the best, the most artistic photography I've ever seen was done by corporate and annual report photographers. The really good ones make the commonplace, like factory equipment, look like some abstract sculpture. They can light under the worst lighting conditions and make miners look like heroes. It is this type of photography, which moves out of the mundane and into the artistic realm, that will convince the guest coordinator to put you on TV where you can discuss and show your art.

Most industrial photographers also do executive portraiture. If they've photographed big names, like Lee Iacocca or Bill Marriott, those photographs would certainly be more promotable than even the more artistic ones of factories.

Editorial

With unique photographs, you should be able to get some coverage in a consumer magazine. Editors are always open to article suggestions, but again, what will sell you is the photographs.

I'd contact the magazines in this order: *American Photographer*, *Popular Photography*, *Modern Photography*, *Petersen's Photographic*, and *Photographer's Forum*. In the trade area, try *Photo/Design*, *The Rangefinder*, and *Photo District News*.

Camera Company Promotion

Corporate and annual report photographers travel the world photographing for their clients. They could be shooting in a Kentucky coal mine one day and at an oil platform off the coast of Norway the next. This makes for some interesting assignments.

If an upcoming assignment is unusual enough, a camera company might give you a specialized piece of equipment with which to do the assignment, in return for the use of some of your pictures for promotion. As long as the pictures you supply them with have already sold, it's a good deal.

Whatever you do, don't give the public relations agency shots that you eventually intend to sell, because, as stated earlier, press releases are widely circulated to the media. Once your shots are widely published, their dollar value will have lessened considerably.

Gallery Exhibits

Consider a gallery exhibit only if your work is really artistic. Approach the galleries in the manner described in Chapter Six.

CHAPTER NINE

Promotion Can't Do It All

One of the most wonderful emotions a professional can experience is that moment of elation when someone calls you for a job. When that call is on the basis of a promotion, whether free or paid, there's an additional feeling of satisfaction for a job well done, and for a faith in oneself that was borne out.

But don't let that exhilaration carry you too far away from the reality. You still have to land the job.

HIGH ANXIETY

No matter how successful you get, you're always going to worry about the next job. That anxiety can have an adverse affect, especially when you really need the work to pay the rent and put food on the table.

How do you control this type of anxiety when so much is on the line? One way is to realize that you're "on the board," so to speak. On the basis of your promotion, you now have a chance to sell yourself to a potential client—an opportunity that previously did not exist. This should add to your confidence and allay some fears.

Another way is to adopt the attitude of Bill Robinson. Robinson is currently the batting and first-base coach of the New York Mets. A former successful major league player, when he's teaching hitting, he tells the players, "It's not your wife and it's not your life." In other words, keep baseball in perspective. The same thing applies to photography.

Long Term Relationships

Compounding this anxiety problem is the failure to look to the future. The tendency is to think about *this* job, not about its long-term ramifications for your career. So in a sense, when you go in for that initial interview with the client, a lot more than one job may depend on the outcome. Of course, this could produce more anxiety, or, the impetus to meet the challenge.

A SELLING TOOL

The potential client will want to see your work, in addition to wanting to interview you. Your photographs are an expression of self and your best, most tangible selling tool.

If you have a rep, you and he or she will have a good idea what it should contain. If not, you'll have to do the portfolio selection yourself.

Generalized or Specialized?

Photographers who are starting out should have a generalized portfolio that contains images from a number of different photographic areas.

You should also build a specific portfolio that features each of the different specialties you work in. The reason is, many clients just want to see the types of photographs that apply to them. They are not interested in photography done in subject areas different from their own.

These specialized portfolios can be broken down as follows.

1. The Editorial Portfolio. Contains images shot for magazines and newspapers.

2. The Wedding Portfolio. Actually different wedding albums shown to potential clients. Each album features formal photographs and candid images taken during the ceremony and reception.

3. The Commercial Portfolio. Contains images shot to promote or sell a product, such as perfume, eyeglasses, or soft drinks.

4. The Corporate Portfolio. Contains photographs taken for corporate brochures and annual reports. Also included are architectural and aerial shots taken for a client rather than a magazine.

5. The Fashion Portfolio. Photographs of men and women, wearing any type of clothes from gowns to jeans, and accessories like belts and earrings.

If you don't have enough shots taken on assignment, then go out and simulate an assignment in whatever category or categories you are deficient in. Get ideas for your portfolio photographs by studying the work of photographers you admire.

Portfolio Size and Arrangement

The portfolio should contain no more than 20 of your top images. The art director or creative director with whom you'll be dealing does not have time to go to a light box or set up a projector to view a lot of images. They prefer a limited amount, which they can evaluate in a more leisurely fashion.

The reason I've emphasized top images is because frequently they have to speak for themselves. The potential client might be too busy to give you the time for a personal presentation. In such a case, the portfolio is dropped off with a receptionist or secretary in his office.

Make sure all of your slides are in color. The exception is when you know, in advance, that an art director is looking for a photographer to shoot a black-and-white ad campaign. In the latter case, you would include black-and-white images.

In addition to current work, the portfolio should include work done in the last two years. You want your portfolio, or "book" as it's known in the trade, to reflect a sense of distinction and continuity in your work.

The chromes should be mounted between black mattes and sealed with tape and glassine. This way, they'll always have an attractive, pristine appearance.

You may also include tearsheets of jobs with which you were satisfied. They should be laminated, with trimmed edges.

Regardless of the way your portfolio is put together, do not show an original shot and then compare it to the final proof. You are not with the client to show comparisons, but rather the scope of your work—the chromes—and how successful you've been—the tearsheets.

Portfolio Cases

The most common way of carrying your photographs and tearsheets is in a zippered portfolio. Zippered portfolios are available in sizes from 8 × 10- to 20 × 24-inches from art-supply houses. Such portfolios are made out of imitation leather, real leather, or fabric. If you can afford it, opt for the real leather one. Leather shows affluence and style and smells great too.

Instead of a zippered portfolio, another option is a box that's encased with one of the materials I've just described. Like the zippered portfolio, the box would contain your transparencies and tearsheets.

DRESSING THE PART

There's a fine line between dressing the way you think you should be dressed and stifling your creativity in clothes selection. Certainly, you should wear what you feel comfortable in, as long as it won't stop you from getting the job, which is the primary goal of the interview. That's why, even if you prefer wearing jeans and a collarless shirt, which I do, it's a good idea to go into the interview dressed a bit more conservatively. You can exercise creativity in choice of accessories.

In general, a nice sports jacket, slacks and tie would be sufficient, a suit even better. Make sure that whatever clothing worn is the right weight for the season it's being worn in.

For example, suppose you've worn a heavy gabardine suit to a summer interview. It's sweltering hot outside, you have to struggle through crowds to get to the building where the interview is taking place. By the time you arrive in the air-conditioned office, you're the only one sweating onto the client's desk. Make sure he's got a blotter to soak it up.

Conversely, wearing a summer weight suit to a winter interview will cause you to shiver for the first couple of minutes of the interview, until your body gets acclimated to the indoor temperature.

I've always found during interviews that eventually, the interviewer's gaze flicks down to my feet. This could either mean that I'm dealing with a lot of people who have foot fetishes, or that they're interested in whether my shoes are shined or not. I prefer believing the latter, because the former might cause me to lose faith in humanity.

Shoes should match in color the outfit being worn. Brown shoes do not go with a dark suit, but cordovan ones do. Most of the time, if you have a pair of black shoes in your wardrobe, they'll go with just about any combination of clothing, except when you're wearing colors in the brown family.

Shoes should always look as new as possible, which denotes affluence. Make sure they're shined and there aren't any holes in the bottom. Don't laugh. I can remember a famous picture of Adlai Stevenson during one of his presidential campaigns when he was photographed relaxing, feet up, exposing a big hole in one of his shoes. He didn't win. Maybe people figured he couldn't afford to fix his shoes.

HANDSHAKE AND EYE CONTACT

Years ago, I was fired from a public relations job. My supervisor told me, "Fred, in this business, you shouldn't be doing what you're doing."

"What am I doing?" I asked.

"You shake hands firmly and look people in the eye. That's no good in this job."

Well, I really didn't argue. I suppose he was telling me not to assert myself or show confidence with the handshake and not to look in the other person's eye because I might not be telling the truth.

The explanation is not important. I still feel he was wrong. The way you shake hands *is* a means of expressing yourself.

Now, you shouldn't try to make it into a macho thing, to see who has the stronger handshake. Just shake hands firmly. This will denote self-confidence and strength of *character*, and while you're doing that, look the other person straight in the eye. That'll show, at least superficially, that you're not intimidated by the client's power. You and I know better; you're probably more than a bit nervous, but don't show it. A firm handshake and a straight look will help you keep up the front.

POSTURE

Posture is another method of judging a person. The person who stands tall radiates harmony and confidence. The person who slumps looks like he has the weight of the world on his shoulders.

Would you want to hire such a person? I wouldn't. He's already too busy worrying about the world.

When you sit, do so comfortably and don't sag down in the chair. That'll make you look like a bored teenager listening to a trigonometry lecture. Just sit comfortably, legs crossed, hands in lap, or whatever other position you find the most relaxing.

I think you should also be aware of body language. Body language is sort of an informal science that tells the viewer, on the basis of the way you sit or stand, what you think about what's going on, what kind of "vibes" you're giving off.

For instance, if you're talking to an art director who's on your right, and you're leaning to your left, he could interpret that you're trying to get away from him. Body language is picked up and is interpreted, so be aware that it is and adjust yourself accordingly during the interview.

INTERPERSONAL COMMUNICATION

Not every photographer can talk to people. I know one photographer who specializes in taking special-effects shots. He's not interested in working with people at all and in fact, has trouble communicating with them. I think this has held him back because while photography can be done without a human subject, a photography *business* cannot be done without extended contact with other people, what communicators term interpersonal communication.

More than any other factor, the way you communicate will determine whether you get the job or not. The way you express yourself is an indication of your understanding of the client's needs and the manner in which you're going to execute the job.

Let's begin with arriving to see the potential client. You check in at the receptionist's or secretary's desk, tell her you have an appointment with Mr. Smith. She gets him on the phone, and you sit down to wait. Those couple of minutes stretch into a half hour. This is not uncommon, especially when seeing someone for the first time.

But you don't think about the logic. All you can think about is you went through all these preparations for the interview and the guy is keeping you waiting. You get angry. Maybe you're also angry because someone else in your life keeps you waiting. You use this opportunity, since they're not in the office, to transfer the anger to the person you're seeing. By the time he appears, offering profuse apologies for his tardiness—also common—you're looking at somebody who is not himself, but the physical embodiment of the other person who's also a late arrival. You're tense and you mumble your hellos and are stiff with anger the rest of the interview.

Guess what? You lost the job before you got in the door of his office. People pick up on anger easily and it turns them off. Nobody wants to work with someone who evinces hostility.

How do you avoid this scenario? First off, you have to expect that you'll be kept waiting. You're there to be interviewed for a job. The other person is holding the cards and you have to play by his rules until you're in more of a position to assert your rights. Sometimes, the person might just be testing your patience. Show your anger, show your *emotion*, and you fail.

The second thing to keep in mind is that the person is an individual. He does not represent anyone else. When you're angry at somebody, but use the present situation to displace that anger onto someone else like the potential client, you're exhibiting a neurotic response that psychological therapists call *displacement*. The way to avoid this is to remain in control of your feelings and thoughts when you're under pressure and waiting in that outside office. If you start thinking of someone else you're angry at, *be aware of it*. If you then turn the anger from that other party toward the potential client, you'll be able to say to yourself something like, "I am angry at the potential client for keeping me waiting, but my anger isn't justified by the situation. I'm really more angry at my friend, who kept me waiting for dinner last night." Once you do this, you'll calm down and when the potential client finally appears, you'll be set for the interview.

THE INTERVIEW

Now that Smith has appeared and you've shaken hands, he leads you through a labyrinth of offices. You'll probably be making small talk along the way. Don't try to be glib and impress him with your witty repartee. Just follow along and respond in kind and try not to laugh too nervously at his jokes.

When you reach his office, he'll offer you a seat. As you're getting seated, take a look around his office. See if there's anything of special interest, that you can use as a conversation breaker. I did an interview with photographer Burt Glinn once, where I noticed some old copies of a magazine he used to work for under a desk. When I asked him why they were there, he told me how much he'd enjoyed working as an editorial photographer, which was enough of an ice breaker to get into the interview easily.

By beginning the conversation, you'll feel more comfortable, more in control, and you might find something the two of you have in common that will loosen up Mr. Smith as well. For instance, let's say he has a model of a sailboat placed prominently on his desk. You've sailed a couple of times and feel comfortable enough to make note of the model. There ensues a brief conversation about sailing and Mr. Smith realizes you're just a little bit more than a photographer looking for a job.

A few minutes after the initial conversation, Mr. Smith will probably begin explaining the job he has you in mind for. Once he does this, pay particular attention to his words. You should be concentrating, not too hard so your face scrunches up or you have some outward type of reaction, but enough to show your interest.

As he speaks, do not interrupt him. He's trying to convey ideas to you and if you stop him, even for the most intelligent question, the flow will be interrupted abruptly. Wait for a lull in the conversation, or when he's finished his explanation and is eliciting a response, to offer your question or comments.

This the most important part of the interview. The job has been explained and you have to respond. How to do it? The best way is to offer him some preliminary suggestions, specifically photographic solutions to the job he has you in mind for. He'll be evaluating your ability to think on your feet, in essence, your creativity, so just go with your gut reactions. After that, if you can, relate the present job to something you've done in the past that required a similar photographic solution. You'll be giving the impression that you're a talented photographer who's used to responding to a client's needs.

Don't bring up your portfolio, which you've had by your side all along. Let him bring it up. Think of it as an ace in the hole, the "card" that will win you the "pot," the job. You don't show your ace until it's necessary and that's what you do here: let him ask to see the portfolio and when he does, present it to him by opening up the box or unzippering the portfolio and passing it over.

Now, another hard part: just sitting there and trying to look unperturbed while someone else looks at your work and decides whether to hire you. He may have questions, which you answer politely. If there's a particular image or images you're proud of, there's nothing wrong with pointing them out. But don't volunteer any technical information unless asked. Let him make the next move.

After viewing the portfolio, the rest of the interview is downhill. The potential client might say you've got the job and negotiate a fee. He might say he wants to think about it before giving you the assignment. What he probably won't say is he's not interested, not because he isn't, but because it's too awkward to reject you in person. He'd rather do it over the phone or ignore you completely.

Chances are, you're not going to get a definite answer. This doesn't necessarily mean you've lost out. He may want time to think about it, to view other photographers' portfolios or, as I said, he doesn't want to reject you in person. Simply thank him for his time and ask him to be in touch.

I said earlier that the primary goal of the interview is to get the job and that the secondary goal is to establish a long-term relationship with the potential client. Ironically, this will be of immediate importance if you don't get the job.

Bear in mind that you now have a good contact. If you've made a good presentation, the lines of communication are open. Mr. Smith might be interested in you for a future job, so don't let a possible first rejection discourage you. It's no reflection on you. Perhaps your photographic style didn't match what he had in mind for the job, but it may match a *future* job that he's handling.

FOLLOW-UP

If Mr. Smith has told you that you got the job, go out and celebrate. If he's indicated that he'll let you know, it's time to do some follow-up.

Write a letter to Mr. Smith on your letterhead. Date it the same day as the interview for immediacy. In the body copy, thank Mr. Smith for seeing you. Tell him that you really keyed into his ideas and would welcome the opportunity to execute them. Close with a line like, "If you have any questions, do not hesitate to call," and then a "sincerely" and under that, your signature (see sample letter).

Send it out regular mail. Return receipt would be pushing it and the last thing you want to do right now is put pressure on him for a decision. You'll do that if he fails to contact you, by phone or in writing, within two weeks of the interview. If he doesn't respond, call him up and be polite to the receptionist, asking to speak to Mr. Smith. If she asks what it's about, just say it's about a job you discussed.

Now you're about to find out how honest Mr. Smith is. If he is, he'll take the call. If not, not only won't he take the call, he won't return it. Someone might be pressured by deadlines and unable to speak at the moment, but if they don't return the call at all, they're telling you "no."

If you get him on the line, be casual in your conversation, as casual as possible when you really want a job, but do keep the anxiety out of your voice. If he says "no," tell him you appreciate his honesty and you'll call him in a few months when you have some new images to show him.

If he tells you he's still considering you, try to push him a little. Tell him, and be very careful how you put this, that you have some new work coming in for one of your clients, that you're making out your schedule for the next few weeks and you'd appreciate it if he'd let you know if you got the job.

Be sure to say ". . . if I got the job." By using plain language, you're putting it right on the line, telling Smith you're not afraid of rejection. You're also telling him your talents are wanted elsewhere. Both are powerful inducements for getting jobs.

This is a strange paradox. Normally, you'd think that a client would reject someone if he shows power. In my experience, it's not true. Exhibiting confidence elevates your personal stock in his eyes. He'll think you that much better a photographer when your services are in demand and you're not afraid of saying that.

The client has no way of knowing how much in demand you are, so don't be afraid to exaggerate to get the job. Just be sure that you can execute if you get the assignment.

EXECUTING THE JOB

When you get the job, be sure you understand what it is the client wants, then execute it, on time, on budget, and to the limit of your abilities.

It's especially wise when dealing with a client for the first time to give him more than he wants. Go out of your way to exercise a little more creativity. Show him that you're not some assistant who simply does what he's told, but adds a certain measure of his creative personality to the project. Do this and not only will he be thoroughly satisfied, he'll come back again and again to take advantage of your photographic expertise.

The text of the letter to Mr. Smith might read something like this.

June 6, 1986

Mr. John Smith
Laramie Advertising
Laramie, Wyoming 11345

Mr. Smith:

Thanks for taking the time to meet with me today, in reference to the photo assignment that we discussed.

From our discussion, I understand the type of photographs you're looking for. I'd welcome the opportunity to execute them.

If you have any questions, do not hesitate to call.

Sincerely,

Robert Fuller

APPENDIX

FREE PROMOTION WORKSHEETS

What follows is a summing up of the free promotional programs described in this book. Use them as a guide, and to further outline promotional programs that meet your individual requirements.

PROMOTIONAL PLAN ONE

WEDDING AND PORTRAIT PHOTOGRAPHERS

Elements in the following order.

1. *Editorial*

Because it's relatively easy to arrange, this is a good place to begin. Layouts and profiles are good for prestige and can be used as a mailer to previous and prospective clients.

2. *Speaking Engagements*

A secondary source of income that also establishes credibility. PPA members get points toward their credential as masters of photography, which is then used as an additional pomotional tool to the public.

3. *Camera Company Promotions*

Opportunity to borrow equipment free of charge or get it gratis. *Additional bonus of having your name associated with a quality product, which then provides you and your business with publicity.*

4. *TV Appearances*

Especially useful during the fall, when brides are booking for the summer and during the summer, when weddings are taking place and brides are looking to book photographers at the last minute.

5. *Gallery Exhibit*

Additional—though limited—revenues by selling your work at local galleries.

PROMOTIONAL PLAN TWO

COMMERCIAL PHOTOGRAPHERS

Elements in the following order.

1. *Endorsements*

The jackpot, and as such, the most difficult. But endorsements are lucrative and establish the photographer as an expert around the country.

2. *Camera Company Promotion*

A second choice to an endorsement, where you deal with the PR agency instead. Can also be lucrative in terms of free publicity and the loan of equipment or receipt of equipment gratis.

3. *Editorial*

Try for the consumer photography magazines first for maximum visibility and, if that doesn't work, try the trade photography magazines.

4. *Gallery Exhibit*

Doesn't provide the publicity that editorial does, but a good secondary place to show your work to clients and prospective clients with the additional benefit of possible sales.

5. *TV Appearances*

Especially useful in promoting a gallery exhibit. Also, you can promote yourself as a photography expert.

PROMOTIONAL PLAN THREE

PHOTOJOURNALISTS

Elements in the following order.

1. *Camera Company Promotion*

Use an upcoming assignment as a way to get a camera company's PR machinery behind you. Free equipment and extensive publicity can result.

2. *Editorial*

Placed second because of the frequency with which photojournalists are covered in the photography magazines.

3. *TV Appearances*

Pictures of celebrities and war-torn areas, in particular, lend themselves to TV's vast appetite for titillation and stimulation.

4. *Pictures of the Year Contest*

It won't necessarily change your life, but a win here is good for publicity from the sponsoring camera company, as well as making you feel good because you won the most prestigious photo contest for photojournalists.

5. *Gallery Exhibit*

A way to supplement income, while having the general public, who might not see the publication for which you shoot, have an opportunity to view your work. Also good for additional publicity.

PROMOTIONAL PLAN FOUR

FASHION PHOTOGRAPHERS
Elements in the following order.

1. *TV Appearances*
Because this area of photography utilizes beautiful women as models, it's eminently marketable to TV, which loves sexual elements in its programming.

2. *Endorsements*
Fashion photographers may have some difficulty in this area, because the public identifies with more "down-to-earth" pros. But the glamour aspect of the business might carry the day.

3. *Gallery Exhibit*
Again, the nature of the photographs, utilizing beautiful women, and the striking graphics and color in beauty photographs, should make it relatively easy getting a gallery exhibit.

4. *Editorial*
Once again, the subject matter and the beautiful nature of the photographs will carry the day. Magazines love to publish good pictures by fashion photographers.

5. *Camera Company Promotion*
The hook here is the beauty and glamour popularly associated with the business.

PROMOTIONAL PLAN FIVE

CORPORATE AND ANNUAL REPORT PHOTOGRAPHERS

Elements in the following order.

1. *TV Appearances*

You don't see many annual report and corporate shooters on TV which is exactly why I'm listing it first. The unique artistry of the corporate and annual report photographer, coupled with photos of prominent people he may also have taken, are the essential promotional elements to emphasize with the TV show's guest coordinator.

2. *Editorial*

Unique photographs always sell. A good place to get a layout or profile to laminate and add to your portfolio.

3. *Camera Company Promotion*

Promote yourself to the camera company on the basis of an interesting upcoming assignment. You might get a specialized piece of equipment to use on loan or gratis.

4. *Gallery Exhibit*

Only if your work is really artistic should a gallery exhibit be considered as a promotional tool. That's why it's listed last.

PAID PROMOTION WORKSHEETS

The worksheets on the pages following summarize the paid promotional programs described in this chapter. They should be viewed as a guide in tailoring paid promotional programs to your own, particular needs.

PROMOTIONAL PLAN ONE

WEDDING AND PORTRAIT PHOTOGRAPHERS

Elements in the following order, keyed into the seasons of the year.

1. *Fall*

Promotions involving team and wedding photography. It's in the fall that brides book photographers for the spring and summer months and teams form for the coming season. Use a brochure to promote team photography, which will make you look like a successful businessman, the image you want to project. To promote weddings, saturate your neighborhood with flyers, which can also be sent by direct mail to previous and prospective clients.

2. *Winter*

A good time to promote the portrait photography aspect of your business. This is done with a brochure containing executive portraits you've shot, and sent to companies in your area. Also, capture the business of graduating seniors by placing ads in local papers, as well as student publications.

3. *Spring*

This is the season to promote the other types of photography you do. For instance, put together an ad of your commercial and advertising shots for one of the less-expensive regional directories.

4. *Summer*

Summer is the time when people are taking their clothes off to escape the heat and it's a good time to promote boudoir photography. Take out ads in local papers advertising yourself as a boudoir photographer.

PROMOTIONAL PLAN TWO

COMMERCIAL PHOTOGRAPHERS

Elements in the following order.

1. *Graphic Designer*

Get a package price from a graphic designer to design at least three different promotional elements, such as mailers, ads, and posters.

2. *The Hit List*

Compile a specific list of the potential markets you want to receive your promotion and send it to them.

3. *Follow Up*

Keep a written record of who received the promotion, then contact them by phone to make sure they received it. Set up an appointment to show your portfolio to interested parties.

PROMOTIONAL PLAN THREE

PHOTOJOURNALISTS

Elements in the following order.

1. *Posters*

You can impress your market, magazine and newspaper editors, with a poster depicting some of the famous people you've photographed.

2. *Calendars*

A promotional item like a calendar would contain shots corresponding to each month. This way, your photographs would literally be in front of the editor constantly, reminding him what a good photographer you are and that you're someone he should employ.

3. *Ads*

Buy a page in one of the directories. Frequently, art directors need photographers with a specialty in shooting people, like photojournalists, to shoot a job.

PROMOTIONAL PLAN FOUR

FASHION PHOTOGRAPHERS
Elements in the following order.

1. *Graphic Designer*
Hire a graphic designer to give all your promotions a professional quality.

2. *Mailers*
As with other promotional items, mailers should be directed at art directors and art buyers. Mailers keep your name out there and remind these people that you're alive. They are the absolutely essential for fashion photographers.

3. *Brochures*
Brochures are an excellent way to present your photography in a portfolio format.

4. *Posters and Calendars*
Art directors like to receive calendars and, in particular, posters from photographers. The latter can become a wall decoration, but both are constant reminders to the potential client of your photographic excellence.

5. *Catalogs*
This is actually a paid job subsequently used for self-promotion.

6. *Follow Up*
All paid promotions should be followed up with calls to the people they are directed at. An aggressive attempt should also be made to show your portfolio to interested parties.

7. *Directory Pages*
After you've printed up your promotional items, buy a page in one or more of the directories to advertise your services.

PROMOTIONAL PLAN FIVE

CORPORATE AND ANNUAL REPORT PHOTOGRAPHY

Elements in the following order.

1. *Directory Pages*

Since corporate and annual reports photographers are hired by major companies to shoot brochures and annual reports, the best place to advertise is going to be American Corporate Showcase. *The market for this publication is so specific that all the people you want to see your ad, namely the designers of annual reports and brochures, will.*

2. *Brochures and Mailers*

Unless you have a lot of shots of people, scenics, or other easily marketable photographs, the corporate and annual report photographer who specializes in shooting inanimate objects will be best off steering clear of calendars and posters and concentrating his efforts on brochures and mailers, which best demonstrate their photographic and creative capabilities.

INDEX